Lucia E. Roesel-Parent
Debbie Bruce

Beagles

Everything About Purchase,
Care, Nutrition, Handling,
and Behavior

BARRON'S

2 CONTENTS

Considerations Before You Buy 5

Is a Beagle Right for You? 5
Space Considerations 7
The Dog Trade 7
Selecting a Breeder 8
Selecting a Puppy 11
Microchips 18
Taking the Puppy Home 21
HOW-TO: Basic Training 22

Basic Rules of Beagle Care 27

Getting the Puppy Settled 27
A Private Spot 27
The Doghouse 29
The Run 31
Boarding Kennels 31
Traveling with Your Beagle 32
The Security Room 33
Toys—Good and Bad 33
Beagles and Children 34
HOW-TO: Choosing Equipment 36

Grooming 39

Care of the Teeth 39
Foot Care 40
Care of the Nails 40
The Ears 42
Fleas 43
Lice 43
Ticks 44
HOW-TO: Coat Care 46

The Proper Diet 49

History of Dog Food 49
Protein 51
Fats and Oils 51
Carbohydrates and Fiber 52
How to Choose a High-Quality Commercial Dog Food 52
Variety Is the Spice of Life 53
How Many Times a Day? 54
Dry, Semi-Moist, or Canned Food? 54
Raw Meat and Bone Diets 54
Feeding Your Senior or Overweight Beagle 54
Water 55

If Your Beagle Gets Sick 57

Disorders of the Coat and Skin 57
Disorders of the Digestive System 58
Worms 59
Kennel Cough 62
Vaccinations 62
Canine Diseases 64
First Aid 68
Temperature and Heart Rate 70
Euthanasia 71

Obedience Training Using Markers 73

Body Language vs. Words 77
YES Marker or Clicker Mark 77
Jackpotting Rewards 78
Distractions 78
Targeting 79
Luring During Marker Training 79
Baby Steps 80
When to End a Training Session 80
Teaching Sit 81
Look 81
Teaching Down 81

Understanding Beagles 83

History 84

Beagles for Work in
the Field 87

Beagle Shows 88

Information 92

Index 94

CONSIDERATIONS BEFORE YOU BUY

There are many good reasons to acquire a Beagle. Just be sure this popular hound will be right for you.

Is a Beagle Right for You?

A Beagle is not an easy pet to keep. It requires a lot from you. You have to remain devoted for 12 to 15 years or more and provide constant good, and therefore expensive, care.

If other people will be involved, you have to be sure that they are emotionally and physically prepared to take on a Beagle and understand what will be required of them. The person who will bear the primary responsibility for the chores of maintaining the dog should get first consideration.

If the decision to buy a puppy isn't properly made, the dog is going to be the biggest loser. Generally what happens is that the poor puppy is sent from one family that is not prepared to care for it to another equally unprepared family. It winds up unhappy and untrained.

One Beagle or Two?

Another point to consider may surprise you: perhaps you ought to get *two* Beagles! Remember, Beagles are pack dogs. If you think that your work or other duties may keep you from spending enough time with your dog, two dogs may help solve your problem! Truly, two Beagles don't make much more work than one. Here again, the deciding factor may be whether you have enough space, money, and the like.

Male or Female?

How do we pick a puppy? Should it be a female or a male? Males generally grow up to be larger and tougher.

Males are generally more independent and can be headstrong now and then. Also, males are more watchful. Don't be surprised, however, if your male Beagle quickly warms up to a stranger. He may bark a few times, but then he will start wagging his tail and seem to say, "I don't know you, but I sure would like to be your friend!"

The independent spirit of Beagle males can be real trouble, especially if a female in heat

══ T I P ══

Establishing Lifelong Habits

The time to start training your puppy is when you first bring him home. Develop good habits in your dog from the very first day. Do not let bad behavior slide because he is a cute puppy, there will come a time when the bad behavior will not be cute. It is easier to be strict first and relax later than the other way around. Be sure to show your puppy what you want him to do, rather than getting upset at him for bad behavior.

(*estrus*) is in the neighborhood. The odor pulls him irresistibly to the home of the female, where he may spend hours, even days. Generally, this goes along with a miserable-sounding mating call. This attracts other males, who may fight with any other male dogs who are present. The owner of the female will also object to the unwelcome attention. For the safety and security of your dog it is best to not allow him to visit neighboring females in heat by keeping him leashed or in a secure kennel or yard.

Female Beagles tend to be gentler than male Beagles. If you have two or more females who live together, they may have occasional serious squabbles with each other.

When you are picking your puppy keep in mind that a puppy's personality is dependant on the individual; some males may be very gentle and mellow while some females may be dominant and rowdy.

It is easier to keep a female at home. Females are more likely to roam when they are in heat, and most of them are in heat only twice a year. At that time, there will be some bloody discharge from her vulva for seven to ten days. You may want to get specially made sanitary napkins or regular baby diapers with a hole cut for the tail, or you can make do by washing the bedding in the sleeping basket more frequently. If the discharge soils the carpet and furniture, you will have to get sanitary napkins or diapers.

While hormone injections have been given to control estrus in the past, the consensus today is that this treatment poses a danger of inflammation and infection, and should be avoided. The best way to deal with your dog's reproductive system is to eliminate it by spaying or neutering. Puppies are a big responsibil-

ity that should not be assumed by accident. If you are not actively planning to breed your pets, they should be spayed or neutered after they have reached maturity.

Space Considerations

Don't consider just yourself, consider your dog when you think about space. You want your dog to be happy. If you have a one-bedroom apartment on the tenth floor, you don't buy a Great Dane, Doberman pinscher, or German shepherd. I'm not just referring to physical space alone. Quality space is important too.

The ideal situation is to give your Beagle a fenced-in yard. Still, if you live in an apartment, you can find ways to indulge your desire to keep a Beagle. Basically, this means that you have to count on walking your dog at least an hour per day. On your days off, you will have to take him along to a park or the beach, where he can run off his energy. Bored, sedentary Beagles can become destructive and noisy.

The Dog Trade

Care needs to be taken to obtain your Beagle from a reputable source. Evidence of good sanitation, adequate exercise, vaccinations, and de-worming are things that should be considered. Vaccination and worming records should be sent home with your Beagle. Be sure you have done your homework and know what qualities you are looking for in a Beagle puppy. The best source is a reputable breeder. Adoption through a rescue group or humane society is an excellent alternative.

After you have determined the source of your puppy, be sure that you acquire the right paperwork, including pedigree and vaccina-

tions. Buy with care and forethought. Don't buy on impulse.

Selecting a Breeder

If you decide to buy from a breeder, consult the experienced hands in your local Beagle club and the representatives of the American Kennel Club. When you have found someone who seems good, take the time to confirm your selection.

Breeders who want only to sell puppies and show no interest in what you want to do with the puppy after you buy it are not the kind you should deal with. Expect the breeder to ask about the makeup of your family, your housing, and your plans. You may find that the breeder seems reluctant to sell if you live in a small apartment where it is hard to take walks every day.

Show breeders also take an interest in the quality of the puppy they sell you. They may ask you to take the animal to at least one dog show, so that the breeder's success can be measured by the decision of an impartial judge.

Often, a discussion between buyer and seller leads to a genuinely friendly understanding. That's fine, provided that you don't lose sight of the business aspects of the relationship. You have the right to see the various papers, and the breeder has the obligation to show them to you. Some breeders do this with pleasure and undisguised pride. Others refuse, or look for an excuse. If that happens, get back into your car and take your business elsewhere.

TIP

Worth Asking About

With your veterinarian's consent, you can give chlorophyll tablets to your female dog when she is in estrus. This will help to neutralize the scent of the female secretions that attract male dogs.

A purebred registered Beagle comes with a registration certificate or an application form from the American Kennel Club, United Kennel Club, America's Pet Registry, National Kennel Club, or others. This form must be filled in properly and forwarded to the registry (see page 92). There may also be a pedigree. Understand that the pedigree is only a chart giving the puppy's ancestry. It is not a part of his official papers. The registration certificate is an official document. If the breeder has already named the puppy you picked and has registered it, you must register the transfer and send the certificate with the appropriate fee to the registry. The registry then transfers the puppy to your ownership and keeps a record of it. You receive a new certificate. If the breeder gives you only an application for registration, you should complete it as quickly as possible, giving the name you selected for the puppy. Mail the completed application with the appropriate fee to the registry address on the papers.

Many breeders administer their own puppy vaccinations. Pups are then sold with a health/vaccination record, but not a veterinary certificate. Owners are then encouraged (or required by contract) to have their own veterinarian examine the puppy within three days or so of purchase to confirm freedom from health problems.

You would do well to plan to view your prospective puppy's litter several times. You may be excited about your future pet, but don't make a definite selection before the puppies are seven to eight weeks old. Breeders generally do not require you to select from a litter that is much younger.

Usually, business is done on a first come, first serve basis. You put your name on a waiting list, and your turn comes after the people whose names are higher on the list have had their turn. If your name tops the list, you have the choice of the litter. If you are, let's say,

═══ T I P ═══

Kennel Conditions

The condition of the kennel itself can tell you a lot about the care and attention the breeder gives to the dogs. Don't expect a superluxurious layout and a pressurized cleaning system. Not every breeder can afford this. But if, for example, the place is piled high with manure, look elsewhere for your puppy.

fourth on the list, then you can choose from all but the three puppies that have been sold or promised to another.

When the time comes, be sure you understand that you have the right to refuse to buy. The refusal can be based on a variety of circumstances. Perhaps the puppy doesn't appeal to you, or perhaps you've had another look around the kennel and things don't look right to you.

Your first visit should occur when the puppies are five to six weeks old. Your discussion with the breeder will tell you a lot. You should also pay attention to the female that mothered the litter and to other dogs on the premises. How do they act? Do they look well fed and well cared for? If they look good, the puppies are likely to be good. If the level of care is poor, then don't expect that the puppies will fare any better.

The puppies themselves should be the picture of health. By the time you make your choice, the seven- or eight-week-old puppies should be active and moving fairly fast. Sluggishness is a poor sign, unless the puppies have just finished a meal.

Selecting a Puppy

Good puppies should have meat on their frames, but their ribs should still be evident to the touch. Sunken flanks and protruding ribs point to poor feeding. Round bellies can point to an infestation of intestinal worms unless the pups have just eaten a large meal.

Pay close attention to the body openings. There should be no feces stuck under the tails, a sign of diarrhea. In female puppies, the area around the vagina should be clean, as should the sheath of males. The drooping, low-set ears should also look clean.

There should be no pronounced odor beyond the natural puppy smell. Pay especially close attention to the eyes. They must be clean, wet, shiny, smooth, and transparent. Too much moisture in the eyes is also undesirable. Tears

running down the cheeks are a sign of a possible infection.

Be sure to check inside the ears. A reddish brown to black discharge in the ear canal indicates the presence of mites or infection.

Finally, make sure that the puppy has a shiny coat and a nice color. I think that the tricolors are the most popular, but also attractive are the white with lemon or tan tigering, especially if they have a black nose and deep, dark eyes. Tan-and-white and lemon-and-white puppies are born almost completely white with a faint darker pattern like a jigsaw on the back and head. Tigering can be black marking on a blue ground, too. Other Beagles are solid white, black, or orange.

If you pick the most adventurous puppy in the litter you need to be equipped to handle his personality and energy level. He will be more likely to test your training skills as well as wanting to explore the neighborhood on his own. If your goal is to hunt or trial your Beagle then this personality type would probably be the best candidate. If you want an easier puppy to train for a pet in a family situation look for a more laid back pup in the litter. A submissive pup would be well suited to a quiet, secure home, perhaps with an elderly owner. You need to be prepared for the possibility that any Beagle puppy you pick, regardless of his personality, may have a desire to wander and hunt.

A Puppy Aptitude Test (PAT) developed by Joachim and Wendy Volhard can be used to identify personality traits at 7 weeks of age. The test should be done in an area that is unfamiliar to the pups and by someone the pups do not know. The puppies should be tested individually away from their littermates and the breeder.

━━━━ T I P ━━━━

Kennel Precautions

If you are visiting more than one Beagle breeder in the same day, be sure to wash your hands and shoes, either with soap and water or with antibacterial wipes. This will minimize the possibility of transmitting diseases from one kennel to another.

Puppy Aptitude Test

© Wendy Volhard 2002

Test	Purpose	Score	#
SOCIAL ATTRACTION Place puppy in test area. From a few feet away the tester coaxes the pup to her/him by clapping hands gently and kneeling down and leaning backwards.	Degree of social attraction. Pack Drive.	Came readily, tail up, jumped, bit at hands.	1
		Came readily, tail up, pawed, licked at hands.	2
		Came readily, tail up.	3
		Came readily, tail down	4
		Came hesitantly, tail down.	5
		Didn't come at all.	6
FOLLOWING Stand up and walk slowly away from the pup with your back to it. Make sure the pup sees you walk away. Coax puppy to follow by talking to it and attracting it's attention.	Degree of following attraction. Pack Drive.	Followed readily, tail up, got underfoot, bit at feet.	1
		Followed readily, tail up, got underfoot.	2
		Followed readily, tail up.	3
		Followed readily, tail down.	4
		Followed hesitantly, tail down.	5
		No follow or went away.	6
RESTRAINT Crouch down and gently roll the pup on his back and hold it down with light pressure with one hand for a full 30 seconds.	Degree of dominance or submission. Fight or flight drive. How it accepts stress when socially or physically dominated.	Struggled fiercely, flailed, bit.	1
		Struggled fiercely, flailed.	2
		Settled, struggled, settled with some eye contact.	3
		Struggled then settled.	4
		No struggle.	5
		No struggle, straining to avoid eye contact.	6
SOCIAL DOMINANCE Sit puppy on left side and gently stroke him from the head to back while you crouch beside him talking to him. Continue stroking until cognizable behavior is established—no more than 30 seconds.	Degree of acceptance of social dominance. Pack drive.	Jumped, pawed, bit, growled.	1
		Jumped, pawed.	2
		Cuddles up to tester and tries to lick face.	3
		Squirmed, licked at hands.	4
		Rolled over, licked at hands.	5
		Went away and stayed away.	6

Test	Purpose	Score	#
ELEVATION DOMINANCE Bend over and cradle the pup under its belly, fingers interlaced, palms up and elevate it just off the ground. Hold it there for 30 seconds.	Degree of accepting dominance while in position of no control. Fight or flight drive.	Struggled fiercely, bit, growled.	1
		Struggled fiercely.	2
		No struggle, relaxed.	3
		Struggled, settled, licked.	4
		No struggle, licked at hands.	5
		No struggle, froze.	6

The remainder of the puppy test is an evaluation of obedience aptitude and working ability and provides a general picture of a pup's intelligence, spirit, and willingness to work with a human being. For most owners, a good companion dog will score in the 3 to 4 range in this section of the test. Puppies scoring a combination of 1's and 2's require experienced handlers who will be able to draw the best aspects of their potential from them.

Volhard Obedience Aptitude Test

© Wendy Volhard 2002

Test	Purpose	Score	#
RETRIEVING Crouch beside pup and attract its attention with crumpled up paper ball. When the pup shows interest and is watching, toss the object 4-5 feet in front of pup.	Degree of willingness to work with a human. High correlation between ability to retrieve and successful guide dogs, obedience dogs, field trial dogs. Prey drive.	Chases object, picks up object and runs away.	1
		Chases object, stands over object, does not return.	2
		Chases object and returns with object to tester.	3
		Chases object and returns without object to tester.	4
		Starts to chase object, loses interest.	5
		Does not chase object.	6
TOUCH SENSITIVITY With puppy on left side, take his front foot with your right hand and press your finger* and thumb lightly then more firmly between his toes on his webbing until you get a response. Count slowly to 10. Stop as soon as puppy pulls away, or shows discomfort. *Do not use your fingernail when performing this test.	Degree of sensitivity to touch.	8-10 counts before response.	1
		6-7 counts before response.	2
		5-6 counts before response.	3
		2-4 counts before response.	4
		1-2 counts before response.	5

Test	Purpose	Score	#
SOUND SENSITIVITY Place pup in center of area, assistant makes a sharp noise a few feet from the puppy. A large metal spoon struck sharply on a metal pan twice works well. Do not repeat.	Degree of sensitivity to sound. (Also can be a rudimentary test for deafness.) Prey drive.	Listens, locates sound, walks toward it barking.	1
		Listens, locates sound, barks.	2
		Listens, locates sound, shows curiosity and walks toward sound.	3
		Listens, locates the sound.	4
		Cringes, backs off, hides.	5
		Ignores sound, shows no curiosity.	6
SIGHT SENSITIVITY Place pup in center of room. Tie a string around a large towel and jerk it across the floor a few feet away from puppy.	Degree of intelligent response to strange object.	Looks, attacks and bites.	1
		Looks, barks and tail up.	2
		Looks curiously, attempts to investigate.	3
		Looks, barks, tail duck.	4
		Runs away, hides.	5
STRUCTURE The puppy is gently set and held in a natural stance and evaluated for structure in the following categories: • Straight front • Straight rear • Shoulder layback • Front angulation/Croup angulation • Rear angulation	Degree of structural soundness. Good structure is necessary.	The puppy is correct in structure.	good
		The puppy has a slight fault or deviation.	fair
		The puppy has an extreme fault or deviation.	poor

Interpreting the Scores

Mostly 1's

A puppy that consistently scores a 1 in the temperament section of the test is an *extremely dominant, aggressive* puppy who can easily be provoked to bite. This puppy is *high in Fight Drive*. His dominant nature will attempt to resist human leadership, thus requiring only the *most experienced of handlers*. This puppy is a poor choice for most individuals and will do best in a working situation as a guard or police dog.

Mostly 2's

This pup is *dominant and self-assured*, also *high in Fight Drive*. He can be provoked to bite; however he readily accepts human leadership that is firm, consistent and knowledgeable. This is *not a dog for a tentative, indecisive individual*. In the right hands, he has the potential to become a fine working or show dog and could fit into an adult household, provided the owners know what they are doing.

Mostly 3's

This pup is *outgoing and friendly* and will adjust well in situations in which he receives regular training and exercise. *High in Pack Drive*, he has a flexible temperament that adapts well to different types of environment, provided he is handled correctly. *May be too much dog for a family with small children or an elderly couple* who are sedentary.

Mostly 4's

A pup that scores a majority of 4's is an *easily controlled, adaptable puppy* whose submissive nature and *high Pack Drive* will make him continually look to his master for leadership. This pup is easy to train, reliable with kids, and, though he lacks self-confidence, *makes a wonderful family pet*. He is usually less outgoing than a pup scoring in the 3's, but his demeanor is gentle and affectionate.

Mostly 5's

This is a pup who is *extremely submissive*, *high in Flight Drive* and lacking in self-confidence. He *bonds very closely with his owner* and requires regular companionship and encouragement to bring him out of himself. If handled incorrectly, this pup will grow up very shy and fearful. For this reason, he will do best in a predictable, structured lifestyle *with owners who are patient and not overly demanding*, such as an elderly couple.

Mostly 6's

A puppy that scores 6 consistently is *independent, low in Pack Drive and uninterested in people*. He will mature into a dog who is *not demonstrably affectionate and who has a low need for human companionship*. In general, it is rare to see properly socialized pups test this way; however there are several breeds that have been bred for specific tasks (such as basenjis, hounds, and some northern breeds) which can exhibit this level of independence. To perform as intended, these dogs require a singularity of purpose that is not compromised by strong attachments to their owner.

Developed by Joachim and Wendy Volhard
© Wendy Volhard 2002

As soon as you have made your selection, it is a good idea to ask the breeder to differentiate your puppy from the others in the litter. Depending on the breeder's preference she may use a colored ribbon or string collar, microchip, or ear tattoo. If the markings of each pup in the litter vary enough to tell them apart you could also take a picture of your puppy for future reference.

Microchips*

Implantable microchips are cylindrical devices (about the size of a grain of rice) that are injected under the skin (usually on top of

*My main source for the Microchips topic was an article at *www.avma.org/issues/microchipping/ microchipping_bgnd.asp*.

the back between the shoulder blades) using a hypodermic needle. Microchips are battery-free—activated by a low-power radio frequency emitted by scanners. When activated the chip transmits a unique preprogrammed identification number.

If your puppy's breeder has not microchipped your pup it would be wise to consider having your veterinarian inject a brand of microchip that uses a frequency common in the United States. Currently the majority of chips and readers in the United States are 125-kHz, the rest of the chips are 128-kHz and 132.4-kHz. If the chip used in your Beagle is of an uncommon frequency the scanners found at most veterinarians and animal shelters will not be able to read it and they will assume that there is no microchip present.

Be sure to register the microchip in your name so that your pup can be identified and returned to you in the event he is lost, if you do not register your puppy's chip there is a good chance that you will not be reunited with your lost companion. It is important that you keep your microchip registration information (phone number and address) current. There are several companies that offer lifetime registration with a one-time fee; other companies require a yearly renewal fee. An on-line search will give you several results for well-established companies and their fees and services.

Microchips are very safe for dogs. The main objection cited by opponents of microchips is an increase in tumors. The unified microchip registration database in the U.K. *www.petlog. org.uk/* reports more than 3.7 million registered, microchipped pets. There is no statistically significant increase in tumors between microchipped dogs and un-chipped dogs; the most common adverse reaction is chip migration (to the shoulder or elbow) according to records kept by the British Small Animal Veterinary Association, which instituted a microchip adverse reaction reporting system

in 1996. There were only two tumors reported in chipped pets between 1997 and 2009. It is possible that these may be due to vaccination injections since both are generally done in the same area.

Studies citing high incidences of cancer in microchipped mice and rats should not be a factor in deciding whether or not to chip your Beagle. Mice and rats are more susceptible than other species to developing foreign-body-induced tumors—not to mention the fact that many laboratory mice and rats are strains that are more susceptible to cancer and were exposed to high levels of carcinogens for the studies; assuming increased risk in other species, including dogs, is inappropriate. The proportionally larger size of a microchip implanted in a mouse or rat may also contribute to the higher rates of tumors in those species than in dogs. In addition, the microchips implanted in laboratory animals are not the same type of microchips that are implanted into pets.

Microchip implantation is unquestionably important in reuniting lost pets with their owners, but it should not be a considered a substitute for proper tags or a personal identification plate on your Beagle's collar.

Taking the Puppy Home

The best procedure is to arrange the transfer of your new puppy in advance. That way, the breeder can take precautions that minimize the chance of car sickness. Food should be withheld from the puppy or he should be fed lightly four hours before you plan to pick him up. If you insist on selecting a puppy and taking him with you on the spot, the risk is yours.

If it will be a long trip, take a thermos with water and a watering bowl.

Most reputable breeders will require the purchaser to bring along a safe traveling crate for the puppy to ride in. A puppy loose in your car is a major distraction and can become a flying object should you need to brake suddenly or become involved in an accident. Make sure that the crate is large enough for the dog and that it provides adequate ventilation. The crate should be secured in the car so it doesn't also become a flying object in the event of a sudden stop or accident. A seat/shoulder belt can often go around the front of a crate and be buckled in. There are also specially made straps designed to be used with the existing vehicle seat belts to secure the crate.

You need to take precautions with your Beagle if your vehicle has front seat and side airbags. Do not put your companion in the front seat and be sure to secure his crate or seat belt to leave space for side airbags.

There may be laws in your state requiring dogs to be restrained while traveling in vehicles, be sure to check the laws in your state before traveling with your Beagle.

Most dogs, including Beagles, like to look out of the window during a car trip. For safety's sake, you should get at the pet store a canine harness and seat belt that is designed specifically for dogs.

Some dogs have continuing problems with car sickness. Your veterinarian has medicine for this condition, but it is healthier to get a dog gradually accustomed to riding in a car. Start during the first ride. Have your passenger keep a sharp eye on the puppy. If she notices any disquiet or salivation, stop the car immediately. Let the dog out for about ten minutes, and then resume the journey.

You may have to stop several times during the first ride, but don't let that get you down. The time you take then will pay off later. As soon as your new puppy is used to his new home, you can gradually expose him to more car trips. Start with a short, one-minute ride, then increase it to two, five, and more minutes. This way, most puppies quickly get used to riding in cars and don't get carsick.

Once you get your new puppy home safely, give him plenty of time to urinate or defecate before you take him inside. Your puppy is now part of the family and he is totally dependent on you for his education, feeding, care, management, and housing.

HOW-TO: BASIC TRAINING

Housetraining

All puppies need to be housetrained. This doesn't have to involve a big drama. Just count on spending a lot of time on the project for a week or two.

First, take the puppy out early each morning. Take him to the same spot, a section of lawn or whatever, where you will walk with him. If your pup is less than about 12 weeks old he will have very little bowel and bladder control so it will be best if you carry him to his potty spot, otherwise he may end up having an accident on the way to the door. When he is eliminating on a predictable schedule you will have time to walk him on a leash, rather than carry him, to his spot. While he is relieving himself you can teach him to associate a verbal command with his actions—say something like "go potty" or "hurry up" (something that you wouldn't be embarrassed to say in public), keep repeating the phrase until he is done. With time your dog will learn to eliminate when you say the command. When he is done be sure to praise him lavishly—throw a little party for him. You can give him a small (green pea size) extra-tasty treat to reinforce the good behavior. This way,

the puppy knows what you expect of him when you take him back to the same spot. In the beginning, you should take the puppy there every half hour or 45 minutes. At the very least, count on taking the puppy out after every meal, every drink, and after every nap. There are also between-times when the puppy looks uneasy, sniffs, and walks in circles as if searching for something. Until three to six months of age, bladder control is not yet fully established. Therefore, you must learn to be alert to your dog's needs and the physical signs he gives you.

Elimination should be handled with common sense. Until a puppy truly understands what he is expected to do, accidents happen. These accidents are not evidence of

willful misbehavior, so react swiftly and fairly. To interrupt the puppy if you actually catch him in the process of relieving himself in the wrong place quickly go over to him, say "ah, ah!" to startle him a little, pick him up and take him to the proper spot to finish. Any accident indicates that you need to take him out more often, as well as keeping a closer watch on his body language, so you don't have repeated accidents.

Keep your Beagle puppy on a timely feeding schedule. Offer him food one to three times a day, depending on his age, this way his potty schedule will be predictable too.

Clean each "accident" site to remove urine odor and avoid reattracting the dog to the spot. Use soapy water and a little vinegar or a special solution available at pet stores. Don't use household ammonia, which will only enhance the problem. (Ammonia in urine attracts the dog.)

Paper Training

If it is not convenient to train your puppy to eliminate outdoors, you may wish to use paper training as a temporary measure. In this case, use the urine scent as an aid by saving a soaked wad of paper to remind your pet where the correct spot is.

Start by spreading a large area with newspaper—a small room with a linoleum or tile floor or an exercise pen is ideal. Then, gradually reduce the area that is covered with paper; but be certain to leave a urine-soaked portion behind whenever you replace the paper. In time, you should be able to reduce the "correct" spot to a square yard or so.

Tethering

The easiest way to help your new Beagle learn to do the right things is to tether him to you any time he is out of his exercise pen or crate. Tethering involves attaching a 4 or 6 foot leash to your new dog then attaching the other end of the leash to yourself. I prefer to use a double-ended snap clipped to my belt loop or to a belt. When you use tethering, your Beagle will stay right with you and it is much easier to keep an eye on him so that he can't get into trouble. He won't be wandering into other rooms to chew on your electric cords and slippers, or relieving himself on the carpet. Puppies as well as adult dogs will bond very quickly with the person they are following for several hours a day; it won't take very many days before they will follow you everywhere even when the leash isn't attached to you. By using a clip to your belt you can have both hands free to do other things. When you want

to give your puppy some play time after a successful outdoor potty trip, just let him drag the leash while he plays. If he starts to get into trouble it's easy to just pick up the leash to redirect him. It's important to keep a close eye on your Beagle even while he is tethered to you or dragging the leash; if you aren't watching he can still manage to make a mess right by your feet.

Crates

You need to take special precautions at night and when you can't watch your puppy during the day. You can leave older trusted dogs loose in the house without worry, but you need to guard against a puppy's making a puddle or

pile somewhere in the house. You do this by shutting the puppy in a confined area—a small, uncarpeted room, an exercise pen, or a crate. Suitable crates can be purchased in a pet shop. Don't make the mistake of thinking of the crate as a prison. Your Beagle will accept it as a den—and a den is a safe place for him.

To get your Beagle comfortable with his crate put him in it for short periods of time throughout the day. If he whines or barks ignore him, when he is quiet for even the shortest amount of time let him out. If you reward his protests you will only encourage them, when you reward quiet, calm behavior you will encourage more of the same. Gradually increase the amount of time your Beagle is in his crate. If he needs something to pass the time you can fill a Kong with peanut butter, cream cheese, or other soft treats, freeze it, and then give it to him to work on. You will find that your Beagle will choose to go

into his crate to sleep or to relax. In order for your Beagle to keep the good association with his crate be sure that you do not use it as a punishment when he misbehaves. Leave his food and water bowls out of the crate except at feeding time.

At night before you turn in, take the dog for a last walk and then put him in the crate. Secure the door, and then you can go to sleep.

Maybe not for long! Puppies are used to having their mother and littermates around from the day they were born. They are used to the body heat put out by their family, which isn't available to them now. To keep the puppy warm in his crate, put a hot water bottle inside it. If the bottle is quite warm, protect the puppy by wrapping an old blanket around the hot water bottle.

The puppy is also used to nocturnal sounds made by its dam and littermates. By contrast, your house may be quite silent once everyone has retired. You'll have to do something about that, too. A good method is to put a ticking clock outside the box. That accustoms the puppy to a monotonous, reassuring sound. Some dog fanciers say that the sound of the alarm clock is something like the beat of the mother dog's heart—a sound that the puppy has long been used to.

Place newspapers or an old blanket in the crate. With all that, you will have prepared the puppy for a good, restful night.

Still, many puppies seem to have trouble falling asleep the first few nights. They whine constantly and keep the whole household awake. If this occurs, you may try moving the crate to your bedside. Whether or not this works, be prepared to persevere. It doesn't take all that long to break in a new puppy. After three or four days, he will probably sleep quietly all night long.

BASIC RULES OF BEAGLE CARE

You will probably have a dog bed ready for your new puppy, but before you introduce her there, let her become acquainted with the entire layout of your home.

Getting the Puppy Settled

Everything is new to the puppy, and she will want to investigate everything with her nose and eyes. Several hours may pass before she decides to look for a place to take a short rest. Soon she will be sniffing around again. Don't be surprised if the puppy's resting place is right in front of your feet. Especially during the first few days, the puppy will want to stay in your immediate vicinity.

The intensive sniffing can take several days, because, as I mentioned, the Beagle puppy is a hunting hound. After four or five days, however, the puppy behaves as if she has lived with you for years. She knows all corners and openings and is especially familiar with places where she can look out of a window without losing her balance.

Those first few days, be sure to follow the feeding schedule and menu established by the breeder. If you want to change the diet, don't change it abruptly. Do it gradually over a period of several days to avoid diarrhea.

A Private Spot

If you decide not to use a crate, your Beagle will still need a private spot in your house to which you can send her when you don't want her underfoot and where she can spend the night. Dogs don't have a preference for any particular spot. They accept the space you assign them. You can't, however, keep changing the dog's spot in the house. Dogs are creatures of habit and don't follow if you move their space from here to there.

Choosing a location: There are varied opinions about the best location. People have used a large, well-ventilated kitchen closet, a corner in the den, or the space between two pieces of furniture, like a bookcase and a bench. Any of these is all right with the Beagle, as long

Chew Toys

Provide your Beagle with safe chew toys. Cow hooves, bully stick, and elk antlers are all good for recreational chewing. If your dog is an aggressive chewer do not give her very hard bones—they can cause tooth damage and excessive wear. Many rawhide chews often contain formaldehyde. Nylon or hard rubber bones, stuffed toys, and squeaky toys are fine as long as your Beagle doesn't try to eat any of the parts. If you catch your dog chewing on inappropriate items redirect her to one of her approved chew toys.

as she can be close to her human friends. She wouldn't like a space in a room that people don't use much.

The most important consideration is that the dog's crate or private spot be free of drafts and moisture. Further, the spot should be easy to clean, so provide a removable liner. However, this liner should not be too hard, because this would promote calluses. You need to protect the dog's pressure points, which are the hock joints, the elbows, and the pasterns. An old blanket is ideal.

Don't put the dog's space too close to a stove or heat outlet. I know of a Beagle that had almost constant problems with an earache because she had the habit of lying on the grate of the central heating system. Set it up so the dog will be comfortably warm but not so hot

TIP

The Happy Observer

If you want to make your Beagle really happy, give her a spot up off the floor, where she can see more of the activity around her. Provide space on a bench or an old chair. An old reclining chair is ideal. You can cover it with a blanket, throw rug, or poly fleece. These are simple to launder.

that the difference between inside and outside temperatures is excessive. Bear in mind that dogs generally prefer cooler temperatures than do human beings.

Choosing furniture: Furniture for the dog's spot can be varied. You can use a dog bed, of which there are a variety on the market.

Dog beds are typically made of heavy fabric or fleece that covers an insert stuffed with polyfil or cedar.

Also popular are the snuggle ball-type beds, which look similar to a bean-bag chair and allow the Beagle to create a more body-hugging nest.

The Doghouse

You may decide to house the Beagle outdoors in its own doghouse. A reason for this decision could be lack of space inside your home or a desire to keep the Beagle from constantly being underfoot.

I see no objection to a doghouse, provided you can protect your Beagle from moisture, drafts, and excessive cold. Cold should not be a serious concern. Beagles can stand relatively

low temperatures because they grow a new, thick coat of fur in the fall. You should, however, do everything you can to keep dogs warm and dry at all times.

When building or buying a doghouse for your Beagle keep in mind that canines prefer their dens to be rather small to conserve their body heat in cold weather, so what would appear to us to be a spacious comfortable dog house may be too large for your Beagle. The ideal den or doghouse is just large enough for the dog to stand in and turn around. Ideally the door should be just large enough for your Beagle to step through to minimize the amount of cold air and rain entering the doghouse.

Doghouse Construction

The floor should be at least 1¼ inch (3 cm) thick. Raise it off the ground at least 4 inches (10 cm) with wooden props to permit proper ventilation.

To get the right dimensions for the doghouse, measure your Beagle. The two measurements you need most are height at the withers (the high point of the shoulders) and length, measured between the base of the tail and the withers.

The height of the doghouse should be about one-and-a-half times the height of your Beagle at the withers. The depth should be about one-and-a-half times the length measurement.

Along one side of the doghouse, build a corridor that runs the length of the house. At the back, make a doorway from the corridor into the rest of the house; make the doorway as wide as the corridor with a tall sill or threshold to keep the bedding contined in the sleeping area. The rest of the doghouse is the

Sun vs. Shade

Pay attention to the direction of the sun. Beagles love to sunbathe, preferably on a raised platform. When it gets too hot, however, they seek protection in the shade. You should position the run so that the Beagle can find both sun and shade.

Beagle's sleeping quarters, which will measure one-and-one-half "dog height" by one-and-one-half "dog lengths."

Make the front of the house higher than the rear, so water can run off the roof. Let the roof project over the front of the house by about 8 inches (20 cm) or more. At the sides and the rear, it should project at least 2 inches (5 cm). The roof must be moisture proof. Make it removable for easier cleaning of the doghouse.

Feel free to make the floor space of the house larger if you like. You must certainly do this if the house should hold more than one Beagle.

If you like, you can also build a window into the front of the house. Remember, however, that most dogs look out by pressing their snouts against the glass, so that the window quickly becomes dirty.

I suggest you get a self-closing door for the doghouse, which you can buy in a pet store. The door is easy to install and helps keep the house free from drafts. In cold weather put a thick layer of straw or grass hay in the sleeping area for your Beagle to snuggle into.

The Run

To build a run, provide floor space of at least 24 square feet (7 m^2); the width should be about 1 yard (approximately 1 m) or more. Beagles can move freely inside this space, but there's nothing wrong with providing additional room.

Be sure the floor isn't moist. You have a choice of several floorings: gravel, dry sand, a grass mat, heavy rubber mat, tile, bricks, or concrete. However, the flooring must be cleansed and disinfected, so it is best to choose a substance that is impervious to water. If your Beagle likes to dig–rubber mats, bricks or concrete would be the best choice.

The sides of the run should be constructed using chain-link or heavy welded rod, being tall enough to keep your Beagle in and other dogs out. Some Beagles can easily climb a six foot chain-link fence, if your dog happens to be one of them a welded wire or chicken wire top, fastened securely at the corners and along the edges, will keep her in the run.

If you decide to let your Beagle have the run of your yard you need to make sure that she cannot escape, as well as ensuring that roaming animals cannot get into your yard and hurt her. Installing an underground fence and training your dog to respect the boundaries is a good option for keeping your Beagle in the yard. An underground fence will not keep other animals out of your yard. If there is a possibility that roaming animals could pose a danger to your dog you should always supervise her when she is outside.

Boarding Kennels

When you go on vacation without your Beagle, you must plan ahead. You can leave

the dog with family, friends, or neighbors or ask someone to dog-sit. If that doesn't work, you must find a boarding kennel. Not all of these are equally good, so get a recommendation from fellow members of the Beagle club or from your veterinarians, who may even operate a kennel themselves.

Good kennels are booked early, so count on making reservations for your dog before you make reservations for your own trip. You may have to book space for your dog in November or December if you want to go on vacation in July or August.

Reputable kennels insist that your Beagle's vaccinations be current. Check with the kennel about what vaccinations are required and with

your veterinarian to be sure the vaccinations you have are current. Also be sure your dog is free of fleas and other parasites.

Visit prospective kennels before you make a reservation to make sure that their standard of care is what you want for your dog. Be sure to speak with past customers about the kennel you are considering—obtain references if necessary.

If your Beagle has a favorite bed or blanket and toy take it along with her to the kennel; it will help her to feel more comfortable. You should also take your dog's regular food for her to eat if the food the kennel has on hand is not what she is used to eating.

Even so, your Beagle may eat little or nothing while she is at the kennel. Beagles are devoted pets and they can become homesick. Your dog may look a little thinner when you see her again. Don't blame the kennel operator. If you selected the kennel wisely, the operator will have done the best possible under the circumstances.

In any event, inspect your pet for fleas and flea dirt before returning from the kennel to avoid infesting your home.

Traveling with Your Beagle

If your dog goes along on vacation, make sure that the hotels and motels you book accept dogs. Take along a folding kennel. This is constructed so that it can fit into a small space, and you'll be able to put it into your car.

Some states and most foreign countries require vaccination before they allow your dog to enter. Some even require a quarantine, in which case you'd better not plan to take your dog. Be sure to get this type of information ahead of time. Call your veterinarian, your travel agent, or the consulate of the country you plan to visit.

Take along your Beagle's regular food, feeding dishes, dog bed, blanket, collar and leash, comb and brush, and a first-aid kit. For extended trips make sure you'll be able to get your dog's familiar food en route. If there is any doubt check with the manufacturer of the product you use.

The Security Room

There will doubtlessly be times when a young or adult Beagle must stay at home alone. It may happen every day. Therefore, you should train your Beagle from the first day to be locked into a crate or secure room where she can't do any damage and where she will not injure herself. The first day, put the dog into the security room along with a familiar dog bed and toys. Start with about ten minutes of solitude, and keep quiet during that time. If your Beagle thinks you're around, she will spend all her energy to get to you as quickly as possible. Lengthen the time of solitude by several minutes on successive days until the dog can remain quiet for an entire hour.

The first few days you'll hear howls and cries, but if you make confinement a regular thing, your Beagle will accept it, not as a punishment, but as a regular part of the daily routine. She will learn to amuse herself if you provide a hard rubber ball or a hollow bone or Kong stuffed with treats.

Of course, don't leave a rug or carpet in the security room. The flooring should be tile or wood, so that you can easily clean feces and urine. If there are curtains, be sure they are high off the ground, so the dog can't reach them. Also, don't keep a bookcase with books in the room, because Beagles love to play with and tear at books and magazines. I learned that lesson from bitter experience!

Toys—Good and Bad

It pays to buy proper toys for your Beagle. Veterinarians tell endless stories about strange objects they have removed from the stomachs of dogs, including stones, balls, needles, nails, corks, and rubber bands. As you may suspect, some of these objects can cause all sorts of damage.

Dogs don't swallow objects because they're hungry. They do it in the course of play. You can avoid this problem by furnishing entertaining and safe toys. Many Beagles love to play with a ball, but make it a proper ball. Small balls, like Ping-Pong balls and marbles, are not recommended because they can be swallowed and choke the dog. Don't get a ball that your Beagle can bite through, and don't get one that has a hole in only one end as dogs have been known to get their tongues stuck in them, resulting in serious tissue damage.

Toys made of wood splinter easily and are not suitable toys. Rubber balls and rubber bones are suitable only if your Beagle just plays with them. If she starts to eat them, take them away. Rubber is not digestible and can cause intestinal upsets.

There are many safe dog toys at pet stores. Your Beagle may prefer hard rubber toys or

TIP

Toy Tips

I recommend that you give proper toys to puppies when they are quite young. Toys strengthen their teeth and exercise their chewing muscles.

An old shoe has been used as a dog toy for ages, but I don't recommend it. Tanned leather doesn't dissolve well in the stomach, and if your Beagle swallows pieces of any size, they can cause blockage of the intestines. Further, you are setting up a potentially confusing situation, since your puppy will not understand the difference between an old slipper and your brand-new one! I advise against letting your Beagle play with leather shoes and slippers.

soft toys. There are also interactive toys that require your dog to manipulate the toy to get food or treats; these type of toys are very good for helping your dog pass the time.

Beagles and Children

Beagles are affectionate and adore children. They are wonderful companions, gentle, playful, and even-tempered. In fact, Beagles are also friendly to other pets, including other dogs and even cats. I once knew a Beagle that daily licked clean the ears of a cat in the household; the cat, in turn, groomed the Beagle!

On the other hand, Beagles are spirited dogs, and if they get into conflict with a child, the child may not be able to hold its own. Beagles love to play with children and may even take

the role of protector; this doesn't mean that children can treat Beagles any way they like. Teach your children not to abuse or threaten your family pet. Also, teach them to recognize when the Beagle wants to be left alone and when she invites play. Beagles often make such

A Baby's Arrival

If you are expecting a new baby be sure that you do not neglect your Beagle, continue taking her for walks, playing with her, and training her. When the baby arrives your Beagle will be curious but you must teach your dog to respect the baby's space; there is no need for her to touch the baby (she can see and smell from a distance). Teach your dog that you set the rules concerning the baby and that your little one is to be respected and not bothered. Let the Beagle be with you while you tend the baby so that her curiosity is satisfied in a safe way. Never leave your baby alone with your Beagle—that way there won't be any accidents or mishaps.

invitations, but there are moments when they really want to be alone and left in peace.

For that reason, it's important for you to keep an eye on the situation when a Beagle and a child play together. My point is this: Be sure to teach your children to treat your dog properly.

When you acquire a Beagle, you may be tempted by all the fancy equipment offered in the pet store. Think through your needs calmly, and buy only what you find useful. Here is a list of helpful or necessary items.

✔ A leather or soft nylon collar is necessary.

✔ A leather or nylon leash of normal length—about 6 feet (2 m)—is good to use when you take the Beagle for a walk. Since puppies love to gnaw at anything resembling leather, consider getting a leash with a short section of chain links at the end. At any rate, do what you can to keep the puppy from gnawing on the leash; it's not good for the dog.

✔ Also get a long line (about 15 feet or so) for training or letting your Beagle run off some energy. A piece of clothesline rope with a swivel snap tied on one end is an economical solution that works well, or you can buy a commercially made flat nylon long line. An alternative is a retractable reel type lead.

Be sure that you only use a retractable leash in an area away from traffic and other people and dogs. There have been many accidents resulting in human injuries and dog deaths or injuries caused by the careless use of retractable leads.

✔ Get two dishes, one for food and one for water. Since Beagles are lop-eared, get dishes that narrow toward the top. Get heavy models that can't be upset or pushed away easily. You can minimize having dishes pushed around too much by using bowls with rubber on the bottom.

✔ A metal comb and a brush are also important (see page 47). Also get a narrow-toothed "louse comb." Use brushes with natural bristles.

✔ Get nail clippers, either guillotine or scissor type, or an electric hand-held rotary tool for trimming nails.

✔ Get no-rinse shampoo at your pet store. This can serve as a waterless bath. It is often used for show dogs which may require more frequent touch-up cleaning. It will also provide protection against fleas and other pests. I personally like to use it when the Beagles are still quite small.

EQUIPMENT

✔ A protective spray for the paws can come in quite handy, especially if you take your Beagle for a walk on the sidewalk in winter, with snow on the ground. The spray protects against road salts, and it keeps the pads from becoming cracked and sore.

✔ To keep away all types of vermin such as fleas, mites and ticks, apply monthly Biospot or Onespot-type products. A few drops should be administered topically behind the dogs' shoulders. These products are the safest and most effective means of flea control for a smooth-coat breed such as the Beagle. Flea collars and powders are no longer the preferred method of treating for these parasites, and a number of bloodlines are hereditarily predisposed to having adverse, allergic reactions to these products.

✔ A repellent spray is a good defense when young puppies forget their toilet training. The spray can help wipe out the dirty traces of misplaced feces or urine. To prevent more damage, you can spray in house corners and entryways and on furniture, carpet, certain trees and bushes, and flowers, among other places.

✔ Also important are protective panties made of heavy material to put on a female in heat; they are available in any pet store. This keeps your carpet, furniture, and other household goods from becoming soiled. They come in different sizes; ask your veterinarian for advice.

✔ Rubber massage brushes and/or rubber grooming gloves are essential for grooming your short-haired Beagle.

✔ Get a metal identification tag, either one that hangs from an "S" hook or one that lies flat against the collar. These metal tags should be engraved or stamped with the name and phone number of the owner.

GROOMING

It's no surprise that a well-groomed Beagle is a healthy, contented dog. But grooming involves more than just coat care.

Care of the Teeth

A few weeks after whelping, puppies get their baby teeth. Several months later, these are exchanged for permanent teeth. Generally this causes no problems, but in a rare case, the eyeteeth (canine teeth) don't drop out. You'll notice sharp, pointed baby teeth next to or behind the permanent eyeteeth. The baby teeth must be removed, or they will push the permanent teeth from their place. Take your young Beagle to the veterinarian and have the old eyeteeth removed if they persist beyond the ninth month of life.

Generally, you needn't expect trouble with teeth until your Beagle reaches one-and-a-half to two years of age. After that, you may start noticing plaque, a soft deposit formed by decaying food, bacteria, and saliva. At first it is rather white, but soon the color changes to yellow. Most plaque starts at the gum line, then spreads over the enamel of the tooth. If not removed, plaque may create cornice-like extensions overhanging adjacent teeth but not actually covering them.

Plaque is easy to remove. Brush the teeth from time to time, and the plaque disappears. You should use a regular toothbrush and a special meat-flavored toothpaste, available from your pet store or veterinarian. Don't use an abrasive tooth cleanser. This removes the plaque all right, but also causes slight damage to the enamel.

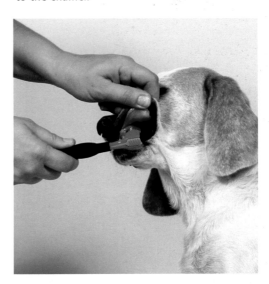

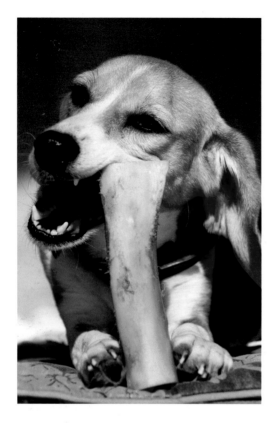

gum. When the gum sticks to objects as the dog walks and pulls on the hair, the dog is in pain. You can prevent this type of scenario by keeping the pad hairs short. This also helps prevent trouble in the winter, when snow and ice can stick to the pad hairs, making the foot a clump of ice. So keep a sharp eye on your dog's pads in freezing weather.

Your dog can get sore pads from small cracks that develop. As long as the cracks stay shallow, they should be considered normal, but if they become deep, you must take action. You don't want your dog to limp or go lame. Start by rubbing the pads with a good baby salve, cod-liver oil salve, or any salve with a glycerine base. If this doesn't bring relief in a day or two, consult a veterinarian. In any case, I suggest you put booties on the sore feet (available at your local pet store) to keep the pad free from dirt until the wounds have healed. Booties will also come in handy for winter walks, particularly on salted city sidewalks and streets.

Care of the Nails

Beagles that walk on hard surfaces usually wear down their nails so that they don't need to be cut. If you keep your Beagle on soft surfaces or don't let him exercise much, the nails tend to grow too long.

Nail clipping isn't hard, particularly if you train your Beagle to tolerate it at an early age. Take a strong pair of clippers—available commercially in several models—and trim a piece of the nail. It's very simple.

Just don't clip too deeply. The nail grows around a tiny cone of connective tissue called the quick that contains blood vessels and

Your Beagle needs to learn at a young age that his teeth are going to be brushed at times. If you don't get him accustomed to this procedure, you'll always have your hands full trying to get the dog to sit still and keep his mouth open.

Don't worry too much about caries (cavities). They don't often occur in dogs.

Foot Care

Check for hair between the foot pads. This hair can cause problems—for instance if the dog steps into a discarded piece of chewing

nerves. When you cut too deeply, you clip off the tip of this sensitive tissue. The dog will jump up in pain, and blood may spurt from the wound.

The lesson is clear: Never clip into the live part of the nail. If the nails are white and transparent, it is generally easy to see where the quick starts. Tissue with capillaries shows with a pink tinge. But if the nails are black or dark, you won't be able to see these signs and you will have to use your good judgment. Some people quickly develop a sense of where to cut and seldom make a mistake. Others err repeatedly.

I advise that you cut only a small bit of nail off at a time. You can be assured that the very narrow part of the nail is not likely to have any quick. If you accidentally cut the very end of the quick your Beagle may flinch and there might be a drop or two of blood; just be more careful when you trim the next nail. With frequent trimming (about once a week) the quick will gradually move away from the end of the toe nail, allowing you to shorten the nails to the length you prefer. After you have cut the nails you can use a file to smooth the edges.

You can also use an electric rotary tool with a grinding drum to trim nails. You need to use caution so that you don't grind off skin on your fingers, as well as taking frequent breaks with each nail so that your Beagle's nails don't get too hot from the friction. Do a little bit on each nail then go over them again until you get the length you want.

If you do tap blood, let the wound bleed for a little while. Then apply styptic powder, corn starch, or press the wound closed with a bandage. When the bleeding stops, put some nonstinging iodine on the wound. If you don't

trust yourself to do the nail trimming right, let a professional do it for you.

There is one instance in which you shouldn't hesitate to take prompt action yourself; that is when your Beagle just about tears out a nail during a fast run or rough play. If you don't attend to a loose nail, it will cause your Beagle recurring pain and trouble. So take the loose nail tightly in your fingers and pull it out with a quick motion. Treat it with a disinfecting wound powder, then cover the wound with a clean, sterile piece of surgical gauze. When the wound is completely dry, you can let the dog go.

A torn nail is quite painful, and you may not be able to clean it adequately without sedation. Antibiotics may also be required to prevent infection. It is wise, therefore, to consult your veterinarian after administering the first aid described above.

If the nail is completely torn out, it does not grow back, although a short stump may develop. You can file this down from time to time to keep it nice and round. This job is really simple.

Dewclaws will require regular trimming. If not cut back regularly, they can become snagged, or grow in a full circle, causing the hound a lot of discomfort.

The Ears

Beagles and many other hunting hounds have hanging or "flap ears" that protect the ear canal against dust and dirt. This is an advantage in the hunt, when dogs have to chase after prey across dusty and muddy terrain. However, the long flaps also require some special attention.

Care of the Flaps

The ear flaps should be washed from time to time, perhaps during an overall bath. It is amazing how much dirt can accumulate along the edges. This dirt is a mixture of wax, dust, sand, and hairs. If soap and water don't get rid of it, use cotton balls or swabs moistened with a little rubbing alcohol. Be very gentle. Also, be aware that this treatment removes all body fats. So follow it up with an application of baby oil.

A problem can arise if a Beagle comes down with an ear infection that causes him to scratch his ears hard or shake them against a chair, table leg, wall, or cupboard. This can cause subcutaneous bleeding (an ear flap hematoma), which needs to be relieved by the veterinarian—an operation that is not at all simple. Naturally, prevention is better than having to cure. If you see your Beagle shake his ears against the furniture, take a close look and be sure the dog doesn't have an ear infection.

Cleaning the Ear Canal

If your Beagle is healthy and his ear is functioning properly, you never (or hardly ever) have to clean out the ear canal. It tends to be self-cleaning. You should still inspect the canal, however.

Start by checking if there is ear wax and, if so, how much. Notice the color. If it is light to dark brown, all is well. Use your sense of smell. If there's a stench, suspect an ear infection. Rub the base of the ear directly behind the juncture with the head. If you hear "sloshing," there is an excess of exudates and perhaps an infection. At the least indication of an ear infection, immediately consult your veterinarian. If you are sure that nothing serious is wrong, continue cleaning the ears. Use an otic solution, which you can obtain from your veterinarian.

Ear Mites

A type of mite (Otodectes cynotis) lives in the dog's ear canal. This ear mite causes an ear infection, which can be detected by excessive wax that is generally reddish brown to black in color. The consistency of the wax generally turns grainy. The infection itches and causes the dog to scratch. As the infection progresses, your Beagle will be in pain. He will hold his head at an angle and shake his ears. Depend on your veterinarian to get rid of this pest.

Fleas

Dog fleas are 0.08 to 0.12 inch (2–3 mm) in size, with the females somewhat larger than the males. They are reddish brown and have six legs.

Fleas mainly infest the neck, the back, the legs, and the base of the tail. They bite the dog, causing an itch. The dog reacts by scratching, biting, and chafing at the itch. A heavy infestation can greatly weaken the dog. It becomes thin and suffers from anemia. Young dogs can even die from a bad infesta-

tion. Furthermore, fleas can serve as intermediate hosts for tapeworms.

Don't delay treatment. As soon as you notice fleas, wash your Beagle thoroughly with an anti-parasitic shampoo. Then consult with your veterinarian for the safest and most effective monthly treatment.

Flea larvae are quite sensitive to moisture, so it helps to scrub the house thoroughly with an insecticide dissolved in water. Pay close attention to cracks and seams in the floor and to wall-to-wall carpets.

If the dog continues to scratch itself, look for another cause. Perhaps there is an environmental or food allergy that is causing a skin irritation.

Lice

Lice rarely occur on Beagles, but if present the veterinarian should be consulted before attempting home treatments; a special shampoo for lice is the usual method of eliminating them, but special care should be taken to prevent overdosing your Beagle with toxins. All flea and lice treatments, along with worming, are basically poisons; their use should be carefully timed to avoid undue stress on your puppy's systems.

— T I P —

The Power of Cedar

Cedar shavings make great bedding for dogs. The aromatic oils of the cedar repel fleas, lice, and ticks.

Ticks

Ticks are arachnids. Males are about 0.06 to 0.08 inch (1½–2 mm) long and reddish brown or black in color. Females are 0.16 inch (4 mm) long and yellowish red.

Ticks hide in low bushes. When a Beagle walks by, they drop down, especially during the summer months. They attach themselves to the skin and suck blood. In a few days, the body of the tick grows to the size of a pea and becomes bluish gray.

Keep an eye open for ticks when you stroke your Beagle and when you groom him, which you ought to do daily, especially in summer.

A tick clamps its mouthpiece into the skin of the dog and is therefore difficult to remove. If

you pull off the tick, the head of the tick can remain and can cause an infection that is quite painful to the dog. The best way to remove a tick is to use alcohol or acetone. Place one drop on the tick's head. Wait a moment, and then you can lift the pest from the dog's skin with a pair of tweezers. Do not twist. Use firm and constant upward pressure. Disinfect the place where the tick was attached. Then, drop the tick into a saucer of alcohol and leave it there for several hours, or simply flush it down the toilet.

Rocky Mountain spotted fever: Dog ticks can transmit Rocky Mountain spotted fever (Borelliosis)—a dangerous disease characterized by muscular pains, high fever, and skin eruptions. Since the disease is endemic throughout North America, anyone who comes in contact with animals and displays these symptoms should see a physician immediately.

Lyme disease: Beagles of any age can contract Lyme disease from a deer tick. This is a serious, potentially fatal illness. If you notice swelling and signs of tenderness around your pet's joints, contact your veterinarian. Should you find a tick on your Beagle or suspect that it has been bitten, consultation is always recommended. If you have been bitten, see your physician immediately. With Lyme disease, timely diagnosis and treatment are essential.

TIP

Lyme Prevention

Vaccinations are now available for Lyme disease. These may especially be recommended for the hunting/field trial Beagles and their owners, as they are considered the prime candidates to be infected. However, you or your Beagle could contract this ailment in a city park or even in a suburban backyard!

HOW–TO: COAT CARE

Washing

Beagles have a different concept of cleanliness than you do. They will lick parts of their bodies from time to time, but they don't go much further in taking care of themselves. As a result, you will have to turn your hand to grooming. Basically, you need to brush the dog regularly, comb him, and wash him now and then.

Dogs secrete sebum, a type of natural lubricant that keeps the hair and skin supple. When you wash your Beagle, the sebum is dissolved and rinsed away. Since the sebum will soon return, no harm is done. Nevertheless, it is best not to wash the Beagle at all until there is a good reason for it.

A good time for a bath is when your pet decides to take a mud bath, rolls in rotting animals, or gets manure on his fur. You don't want to get dirt and stench in the house, so a bath is the only solution. You can also wash the dog

if he is shedding. If you use a lot of water, comfortably hot, you'll help loosen the hairs. Then, when you brush the Beagle while the fur dries, you'll brush out most of the hair, shortening the shedding time.

Use a shampoo made for dogs. You'll find many good brands at the pet store that remove a minimum amount of sebum from the hair. If your Beagle has problems with his coat, ask your veterinarian for a medicated shampoo that can help. Many dog shampoos contain an insecticide that removes fleas, ticks, and other vermin during the bath.

Generally, Beagles like the bath. They enjoy swimming, after all. Some Beagles hate getting water in their ear canal, however. You'll get a hint of this if you see the dog constantly shake his head. So put a good wad of cotton in the ears before you start.

The best place to work is on a rubber mat in the bathtub. Mix some shampoo into a small tub of warm water, then use a sponge or washcloth to work the soapy water into the dog's fur. You will use much less shampoo this way than if you try to wet the dog first with plain water (the natural oils in the hair will repel the water) and then apply straight shampoo. You can repeat the process if your dog is very dirty. If you are treating for fleas or other vermin you must leave the shampoo on for several minutes before rinsing well. Use your damp sponge or washcloth to wipe down and then to also rinse his face and ears. Be sure to rinse all the soap out to prevent skin irritation.

When bathing for fleas, start on neck and head and proceed toward paws and tail to avoid driving the fleas toward the eyes and ears.

Now take the cotton out of the ears and dry the dog. You can use an ordinary hand-held blow dryer. Be sure to brush the coat while you dry it. Brush lightly in the direction in which the hairs grow so that the hair drops down smoothly. Brush one area of coat at a time. When you've covered the whole dog, go over the fur with a comb to detect any small remaining snarls. Loosen these carefully.

Brushing

Generally, your Beagle requires a bath only once or twice a year, but a good brushing is a frequent requirement. After a few sessions, your Beagle will be used to it; he will pull back his hind legs and lie like a prince while he enjoys the grooming. Don't be fooled because your Beagle's coat generally looks neat; a brushing is absolutely necessary. It helps remove any loose hair.

You can obtain a special rubber brush made for short-haired dogs. Pull this through the fur

several times, and you'll collect a good number of loose hairs. Brushing also massages the skin, loosening scaly skin. The scales work their way through the hair and rest on top of the coat, making it look dusty. Just leave the dusty scales there. In a half-hour's time, the dog will have shaken off a good many of them. After that, remove the rest with a damp washcloth. If you want to do a really professional job, use a grooming glove or a chamois cloth.

Always brush from the neck across the back to the tail in strong strokes. Then brush from the neck across the shoulders and along the front legs, downward, and again from the neck along the flanks, across the hip, and downward along the rear legs.

THE PROPER DIET

High-quality foods in proper proportions suitable for canines are an important part of keeping your dog healthy and active into her golden years. Just as with humans, a poor diet consisting of "junk foods," as well as fillers, chemicals, artificial dyes, and preservatives are not conducive to optimal health and longevity.

History of Dog Food

When our dogs' ancestors first began associating with humans they were most likely attracted by the food scraps that were left in and near the human camps; these canines would have hunted on their own for food, as well as eating meat and bone scraps scavenged from human camps. Over the years as canines became domesticated they continued to eat scraps from their human master's cook pots and trash heaps, as they had for thousands of years. While humans were primarily hunter/gatherers, dogs also hunted, as well as eating scraps that people gave them. As human societies became more agriculturally oriented it can be assumed that their dogs also began eating more agricultural products (kitchen/table scraps from fruits, vegetables, and grains, in addition to the meat, bone, offal, and scraps from animals). As more and more humans moved from a rural to an urban lifestyle they naturally took their dogs with them, and as the industrial age progressed people bought more of their food ready-made. It was natural that entrepreneurs would develop ready-made foods for dogs. In the mid-1800s James Spratt, an American electrician living in London was the first to develop and market the first dog food—made of wheat meals, vegetables, and meat. In the 1870s production of "Spratt's Patented Meat Fibrine Dog Cake" had begun in the United States. In the 1950s General Mills acquired Spratt's U.S. business.

In 1907, F.H. Bennett Biscuits Co. introduced "Milk Bone" dog biscuits which were touted as "whole nutrition" made with meats, cereals, milk, liver oil, and vitamins.

After World War I, and with the invention of cars, horse meat was cheap and widely available for dog food, including Ken-L Ration brand's canned horse meat. Until 1968 Ken-L Ration sponsored the pet kennel at Disneyland, known as Ken-L Land. Ken-L ration was purchased by Quaker Oats, and in 1995 the brand was sold to the H.J. Heinz Company.

Dry meat-meal dog food was introduced by the Gaines Food Company in the 1930s. Clarence Gaines marketed his "100% complete and balanced nutrition" by exhibiting his own

Dog Food Study

A study done by the Iams Company in 2001 examined the relationship between animal sourced proteins versus plant sourced proteins as it related to dog body condition and health:

> Adult and senior dogs were fed diets with varying amounts of protein from chicken and corn gluten meal, and their body composition (muscle versus fat tissue) was analyzed. In addition, levels of key blood and muscle proteins were measured.
>
> Compared to dogs fed a diet with 100% chicken protein, dogs fed diets with decreasing levels of chicken and increasing levels of corn gluten meal had
> - decreased lean tissue.
> - increased body fat.
> - decreased levels of blood proteins routinely used as markers of superior nutritional status.

This was independent of the overall dietary protein level (12% or 28%), which was also examined in each of the four test groups.

As dogs age, body composition and muscle-specific proteins decline. Therefore, another study looked at the differences between feeding senior dogs a 32%-protein chicken-based diet, a 32%-protein chicken and corn gluten meal diet, or a 16%-protein chicken-based diet.

Senior dogs fed the 32%-chicken protein, chicken-based diet had better body composition and a muscle-specific protein pattern identical to that in healthy young adult dogs. However, those results were not seen in either of the other two diets.

Pointer at a well-known dog show. General Foods purchased Gaines in 1943.

During World War II, metal used for canned dog food was set aside for the war effort, nearly ruining the canned pet food industry. Commercial dog foods marketed for household dogs and cats needed to be supplemented with meat in order to maintain an Army dog in good working condition. In the Zone of the Interior the Quartermaster Corps in November 1942 authorized the procurement of commercial dog food and additional meat to supplement the diet. Due to wartime shortages and priority allocations dog food manufacturers had trouble producing high-quality products, and as a result of this, in March 1944, the War Department amended the Army's dog food supply and authorized meat as the main component of the dog ration. The Army Veterinary Service at the Seattle, Washington Depot developed a canned dog food using ground horse meat and herring that was supplied to the Alaskan department.

After World War II the pet food industry capitalized on the meat by-products industry for an economical way to produce dog food. With the economy booming people could afford the luxury and convenience of buying prepared dog food (primarily canned food) and sales reached $200 million. For food companies such as General Foods, Quaker Oats, and Nabisco, pet food represented an opportunity to market by-products as a profitable source of income. In 1956 the first dry kibble pet foods were produced, and throughout the 1960s and 1970s companies began to offer different flavors. The 1980s brought about the introduction of ailment-specific diets such as those for kidney or liver failure. In the 1990s pet food diversified to include diets based on activity level and breed of dog. The current trend in pet foods is toward more holistic or natural diets, including raw and human-quality foods. Nutritional research continues to change diet recommendations; as we learn more about our dogs we will continue to improve their diets. The pet food industry has grown to annual sales of over $15 billion, with convenience and price being of less importance to many dog owners than high food quality and their pet's health.

Protein

High-quality protein that is readily digestible for your Beagle is found in various animals including beef, lamb/mutton, goat, venison, chicken, duck/goose, rodents, and fish. Eggs and cultured milk products (plain yogurt and kefir) are also excellent sources of protein. Plant-based proteins are usually derived from soybean meal and corn-gluten meal.

Protein supplies the body with amino acids to build skin, hair, nails, muscles, tendons, ligaments, and cartilage. Protein also plays an important role in hormone and enzyme production. Animal-source proteins contain all the essential amino acids dogs need, whereas some plant-based proteins may be deficient in some essential amino acids.

The digestive tract of canines is short and does not have the capacity to digest large amounts of plant products. Therefore dogs do best when fed primarily animal sourced proteins. If you feed your Beagle a diet that is primarily grain-based there is a good chance that your pet will have issues with excess weight and less than ideal body condition, poor dental health, skin problems, and yeast or fungal conditions.

Fats and Oils

Your Beagle uses dietary fats for energy. Fats can be obtained from a variety of sources, primarily animal fats, fish or krill oil, and vegetable or seed oils. Fats are a very energy dense food, containing twice the kilojoules per gram as carbohydrates and protein. Growing puppies and very active dogs will need more fats than sedentary dogs.

Fats contain varying levels of omega-3 essential fatty acids and omega-6 essential fatty acids. Refined vegetable oils are high in omega-6s. The fat of animals that have consumed mainly grasses and herbs contain a balance of omega-6s and omega-3s. Animals which have been raised in the typical commercial feedlots are fed primarily grains, which causes their fat to be high in omega 6s and low in omega-3s. Omega-3s are widely recognized as beneficial for their anti-inflammatory properties. A balance of one part omega-3s and two parts omega-6s is ideal. Because most commercial dog foods, as well as most available meat, is high in omega-6s it is wise to provide supplemental omega-3s in the form of fish oil or krill oil. These oils are available in liquid or capsule form; the capsules will keep their freshness longer than the liquid because the capsule prevents air contact, which causes the oil to go rancid. If your dog won't eat capsules (most dogs love them) you can buy the liquid form or puncture and squeeze the capsule onto her food. As well as supplementing with fish or krill oil, you should also give your dog Vitamin E to protect her from free radicals present in any rancid oils or fats in her diet. If you feed your Beagle a diet high in grass-fed animal products then you probably don't need to supplement with omega-3s and Vitamin E, unless there are health concerns such as skin and joint problems.

Carbohydrates and Fiber

Dogs have a short, simple digestive tract, well suited to foods that can be quickly digested, such as proteins and fats. Carbohydrates can be digested to some degree and will give your Beagle a boost of quick energy. Carbohydrates in the form of grains and potatoes are added to dog foods because: these ingredients are usually lower priced than meat, they are used as a binder in extruded kibble, and they act as fillers to make to dogs feel full after a meal. Carbohydrates and fiber from grains and vegetables in their natural forms will largely pass undigested through the gut; therefore they must be processed to allow dogs to digest them. Vegetables are generally added to dog foods to add vitamins and minerals to the dog's diet, as well as to help the dog feel full. Grinding, puréeing, or cooking are methods used to make vegetables more nutritionally available for dogs.

Fiber is added to commercial dog foods in the form of beet pulp, soy hulls, or grain hulls in order to bulk up the food and to make the dog feel full; however, because of the dog's short digestive tract it is not digested and will increase stool volume.

How to Choose a High-Quality Commercial Dog Food

The main ingredients in dog food are the first five listed on the label; they will indicate the quality of the food. Meat or meat products should ideally make up the bulk of the main ingredients, followed by fats, vegetables, and grains. Growing puppies and very active adult dogs will need a food with a higher fat content relative to the protein. Human grade and organic ingredients are used in many of the better quality foods. Choose foods with named sources of fats and proteins such as beef fat, chicken fat, or lamb meal. Generic sources of fat and proteins such as "meat meal," "meat and bone meal," or "animal fat" are indications of a poor quality food. Corn gluten meal is often included in lower quality foods and provides incomplete protein for dogs, so it should be avoided. It is best to avoid foods with artificial preservatives such as BHA, BHT, Ethoxyquin, and Propylene glycol. Natural preservatives that include Tocopherols (Vitamin E) and ascorbic acid (Vitamin C) are safe alternatives—however, the food should still be used within six months from the date of manufacture. Dog foods with artificial colors, sugars, and sweeteners (such as corn syrup, sucrose, and ammoniated glycyrrhizin) should be avoided.

Compare the feeding guide on the label of each food you are considering; premium foods have a higher nutritional content and will recommend feeding less food per dog than foods with more fillers and less nutritious ingredients. A nutritionally dense dog food will be more economical than brands with lower quality ingredients because you will feed less of it; in addition, there will be less dog waste to clean up.

A high priced or well-known brand dog food is no guarantee of high quality. Before you buy any dog food you should always read the ingredient labels of the foods you are considering for your Beagle.

Variety Is the Spice of Life

You should feed a variety of foods to your Beagle over time. You can choose three or four high-quality foods with different protein sources (such as beef, chicken, lamb, and fish) and rotate to a different one every few months to fill in any nutritional gaps that one particular food or brand might have, as well as helping to avoid developing food allergies. When you change your Beagle to a new food, be sure to make a gradual change to avoid digestive upset. Be sure to reserve one or two novel proteins (such as duck, ostrich, or venison) in case you need to do an elimination diet for allergy testing.

You may add a few cooked meat scraps to your dog's kibble bowl; be sure that you aren't adding so many extras that the calcium ratio in his diet is thrown out of balance. If your dog has digestive or bowel upset you should cut back on the extras until everything gets back to normal.

How Many Times a Day?

Depending on your preferences, you can feed your dog one, two, or three meals a day. Adolescent and adult Beagles will do just fine on a once a day feeding schedule. Puppies younger than three or four months old can be fed twice a day; after that they can go to a once a day feeding schedule.

Dry, Semi-Moist, or Canned Food?

Good quality dry dog food is more nutritionally dense than semi-moist or canned; it is easier to transport and store, and it is generally more economical than canned or semi-moist foods of comparable quality. Semi-moist foods have large quantities of artificial flavors and colors, preservatives, and chemicals which make these foods poor choices for your pet. Canned foods often have better ingredients (more protein and fat, low carbohydrates) when compared to many dry foods. It is fine to feed your dog a canned food diet, or you may want to combine canned food and dry food to improve the over-all quality of the diet or to make dry food more palatable for your Beagle.

Raw Meat and Bone Diets*

Raw meat and bone diets have become more popular with a growing number of dog owners. There are several companies selling prepared ground diets which include muscle meat, fat, organ meats, and ground bone, along with vegetables. Some of the advantages of feeding a raw diet include: happier

*See reference materials at the back of the book for more information.

dogs, cleaner teeth, less "doggy" odor, no grain allergy issues, and smaller, less-offensive stools. When feeding a raw meat and bone diet it is very important to make sure the bone/calcium levels are adequate to avoid osteoporosis. and other health problems. Do not feed raw and cooked foods at the same meal as they digest at different rates and may cause digestive upset. You must learn about how to properly feed a raw meat and bone diet before you start; consulting a canine nutritionist who is knowledgeable about raw meat and bone diets would be the first place to start. A responsible dog breeder who has several years of raw feeding experience can also help you to develop a raw feeding plan for your Beagle. Once you have a good grasp of the ins and outs of a complete and balanced raw feeding program you can buy ingredients from your butcher as well as from one of the many companies that sell ingredients for raw meat and bone diets.

Feeding Your Senior or Overweight Beagle

When you look at your adult Beagle from above you should be able to see a definite waist area between his ribs and hips. When you run your hand along his ribs you should be able to feel the ribs, but not see them. If you can't see his waist or feel his ribs he is overweight. You need to be honest with yourself when evaluating your dog; many dogs are overweight and if you only compare him to all the other dogs you see you will not accurately evaluate his weight. If you keep your Beagle trim and fit you will help him stay healthy and increase his lifespan. There are several things you should do for your Beagle if he is overweight:

1. Exercise (walks, fetch, and other games) will help burn off the extra pounds and build muscle.

2. Choose a high-protein food with moderate fat and low carbohydrates. Protein and fat will both provide energy; too little fat will leave your Beagle feeling hungry all the time, which will make losing weight harder. Carbohydrates provide a quick boost of energy with less nutrition than protein and can lead to weight gain; by limiting carbohydrates and replacing them with protein and fat you will help your dog feel satisfied and lose weight.

3. If your senior dog seems to be thin over the top of his back but he has too much fat on his sides and belly it is from a lack of muscle on his top-line. He needs more protein to build muscle, moderate amounts of fat, and very limited amounts of carbohydrates to help in reducing his excess fat. There are commercial high-protein senior and weight loss foods available for your overweight or senior Beagle.

Be sure to read the labels of available weight loss foods to make sure that there are not large amounts of carbohydrates in relation to proteins and fats.

4. Reduce the amount of food your Beagle eats by gradually reducing the amount of food you put in his bowl each day until he is at a reasonable weight. Free choice or self feeding a Beagle prone to gluttony, as many of them are, is a bad idea; you need to pick up his bowl and only give him access to a limited amount of food once or twice a day. This may be hard with those sad hound-dog eyes looking at you, but you can do it. If your dog gives you a hard time about it you can occupy his time by playing some of his favorite games, going for a walk in an interesting or new location, and hiding little bits of his food in various locations around the house or yard so he has to scent it out at meal times. You can use his food as marker training treats so he uses plenty of mental and physical energy while he eats. Another thing you can do is to feed him a few unsalted green beans or pieces of raw carrot to keep him busy a little longer at meal times.

It is important to make sure you are providing your Beagle with a high-quality food with enough protein and fat so that his nutritional requirements are still met when his food portions are reduced. By feeding your Beagle the proper amounts of high-quality foods, as well as making sure he gets plenty of exercise, you will help him stay healthy and happy for many years.

Water

Make sure that you provide plenty of clean water for your Beagle. Most dogs need about an ounce of fluids per pound of body weight a day. Several things such as weather/temperature, activity level, age, and diet can affect how much your dog drinks. Dogs fed raw meat and bone diets generally need much less water than kibble-fed dogs, as they get much of their fluids from the meat. Working dogs, very active dogs, and dogs exposed to hot summer temperatures need much more water than sedentary dogs. Growing puppies generally drink more water than adult dogs. If your Beagle tends not to drink enough water you can increase his fluid intake by moistening his dry food with water or unsalted meat broth.

IF YOUR BEAGLE GETS SICK

The ultimate responsibility for your Beagle's health is yours, but clearly you can't take care of everything yourself. Your most important adviser is your veterinarian.

You have a broad choice of veterinarians, but once you select one, I suggest you stick with him or her as long as you don't have a well-founded reason for changing.

Be reasonable in dealing with your veterinarian. The fact that you pay for services doesn't give you the right to telephone at impossible hours for a consultation—certainly not if your dog has been sick for some time.

Your veterinarian should be able to expect certain things from you. You ought to have basic knowledge about the health care of your Beagle, including worming, parasite control, vaccination, and nutrition.

Disorders of the Coat and Skin

Beagles shed normally every spring and fall, exchanging their winter and summer coats. Abnormal hair loss does, however, occur as well and can be caused by one of the following: poor feeding, eczema, parasites, a generally poor condition after illness, and hormonal disturbances.

Symptoms can include itch, bare spots, oily coat, and repeated shedding. Ask your veterinarian for the right treatment. He or she will look into the following:

✔ What you feed your Beagle can cause reactions on the skin and coat.

✔ Several types of eczema may be caused by excessive carbohydrates in the diet. In any event, leave treatment of eczema to your veterinarian, who will cut the remaining hair from the affected spots, clean the area, and recommend medication against infection. He or she also may recommend an improved diet.

✔ Another possible cause is parasites, including fleas and lice (see pages 43–45) or worms (see pages 59–62). A much more serious parasite is the scabies mite (*Sarcoptes*), which buries itself in the skin to lay its eggs.

The infested dog scratches itself continuously, resulting in raw bare spots at the elbow, knee, and margins of the ear. If left untreated, the bare spots spread over the whole body.

Parasites must be fought with strong remedies. Your veterinarian will recommend treatment. To avoid further transmission, separate the affected dog from other animals and maintain proper hygiene. The environment must also be thoroughly cleansed; otherwise, the animal will be reinfected.

✔ Abnormal hair loss often occurs after serious illness. It certainly will help to gradually restore the normal condition of the coat with a proper, accurately balanced diet.

✔ Baldness (alopecia) in puppies may be caused by a deficiency of thyroxine (thyroxine is an iodine-containing hormone produced by the thyroid gland to regulate metabolism), resulting from an iodine deficiency in the diet of the dam. In any event, consult a veterinarian for advice. Prevent the problem by feeding a pregnant Beagle properly.

A mother dog may have problems with baldness after whelping, caused by hormonal changes. Again, proper feeding can remedy this quickly.

Of course, should the condition persist after several weeks of highly nutritious feeding, it is advisable that you consult with your veterinarian.

Disorders of the Digestive System

Constipation

If your Beagle doesn't defecate "on schedule," there's no reason to be alarmed immediately. You may feed about a tablespoon of plain canned pumpkin morning and evening to help move things along. You may also need to consider reducing the bone in his diet.

Diarrhea

Diarrhea is caused mainly by various infectious diseases, poor feeding, poisoning, "colds," and intestinal worms. The stools are thin, sometimes mucus-laden, and there may even be blood in serious cases.

Sudden changes in the diet, too little calcium, or too much fat can cause loose stools. Take a look at what your Beagle is eating and adjust his diet as needed.

In a serious case of diarrhea, with mucus and blood, you should always consult your veterinarian. In all cases, be sure that the sick Beagle stays warm enough.

Anal Sacs

The anal sacs have small openings that become visible by slightly curling the anus outward. You can notice the two openings at 5 and at 7 o'clock, viewing the anal opening as a watch. The glands continually produce a nasty-smelling fluid that is stored in the sacs until emptied during defecation. The dog can also squeeze the fluid out of the sacs when danger threatens. In other words, the anal sacs function precisely like the scent glands of the skunk. When the anal sacs do not empty normally, they go from being full to being over-filled (impacted). The dog responds by licking under its tail. If that doesn't bring relief, the animal pulls its anus along the ground. We call this symptom "scooting," in which the animal sits, raises his hind legs, and pulls himself along with his forelegs.

Scooting can also be caused by other problems, such as feces adhering to the anus, undigested grass that hangs partially out of the rectum and anus, and small wounds. To determine the true cause, examine the Beagle under the tail. If the anal sacs are impacted, you can often see a small bump on either side of the anus.

A common side effect of an infection of the anal sacs is a bare back. The affected dog has a terrible itch and scrapes himself wherever it can. Generally the bare spot develops on the rump. This is the same spot that is chafed bare when a dog has fleas. So if you see a bare back, remember to look not only for fleas but also for problems in the anal sacs. If the anal sacs are overfilled, they must be emptied manually—a job best left to your veterinarian. Remember, if this isn't done, there may be all kinds of complications.

Anal sac infections can be cured by medication. Some veterinarians also advise an operation to remove the sacs altogether.

Worms

The most common intestinal worms are tapeworms and roundworms.

Tapeworms

Tapeworms attach themselves with the head (*scolex*) to the mucous membranes of the intestines and absorb nourishment. The head is connected to a chain of segments (*proglotids*).

The segments, each of which contains a large number of eggs, are excreted with the feces.

Dogs can be infested by at least seven types of tapeworms, one of which, the *Echinococcus* tapeworm, is definitely dangerous to humans. All tapeworms live in the small intestine. Every species of tapeworm has a specific intermediate host for its life cycle. These can be fleas, lice, sheep, pigs, rabbits, dogs, or even fish.

The symptoms of tapeworm infestation are obvious only in serious cases. They include weight loss (despite a good diet), excitability, cramps, and sometimes diarrhea. You can detect the segments of tapeworm in the stools as small white pieces. You can also see them as dried pieces resembling rice kernels in the hairs around the anus. Immediately consult a veterinarian. He or she will prescribe remedies against the worm as well as against any fleas present.

Roundworms

Roundworms are sturdy and white, ranging in length from 2 to 4 inches (5–10 cm), with the females longer than the males. They also appear in the small intestine.

The eggs are excreted with the stools. When a dog takes in such an egg, it lodges in the intestine. There the egg develops into a larva, which drills itself through the intestinal wall into the bloodstream, by which it is carried to the lungs. It stays there for some time and then travels via the respiratory system to the throat. It is swallowed and then settles in the intestines, where the larva matures to the adult stage.

Damage to the lungs and liver during the process can cause infections. As symptoms, look for digestive disturbances of all types, changing appetite, constipation, diarrhea, intestinal infections, and sometimes also a vomiting of worms. Pups have a hard, swollen belly; they walk with legs apart, cough, grow thin, and develop a dull coat.

Immediately consult a veterinarian. Prevent infestation by keeping the dog quarters properly clean. Remove feces and disinfect the kennels daily. Examine Beagles regularly for worms.

Hookworms and Whipworms

Hookworms and whipworms are common internal blood-sucking parasites. Hookworms have hooked mouth parts with which they fasten themselves to the intestinal walls of the dog, causing the disease ancylostomiasis. The larvae are activated by the hormonal changes of pregnancy and are carried into the embryos by the bloodstream.

Many infestations occur by way of worm eggs that already-infested animals pass in the stool.

The symptoms of infestation are bloody diarrhea, loss of appetite, vomiting and anemia, and pale gums.

Take the patient to your veterinarian at the first sign of illness (and take a stool sample along in a tightly closed container).

Heartworms

Heartworms are transmitted by mosquito bites and live in the right ventricle and pulmonary artery of the heart of dogs and other mammals. Heartworms, which are extremely dangerous internal parasites, can grow up to 12 inches (30.5 cm) in length.

The signs of heartworm disease include fatigue, labored breathing, frequent coughing, and faintness. Unfortunately, these symptoms are often not apparent until the disease has reached a grave stage. Since large parts of

the United States and Canada are threatened by heartworm infestations, it is now common practice to maintain all dogs on a monthly heartworm prevention program. Consult your veterinarian.

Kennel Cough

Merck Veterinary Manual says this about kennel cough:

> Infectious tracheobronchitis is a mild self-limiting disease that results in inflammation of the upper airways transmitted by air and caused possibly but not surely by several different viruses, mainly Parainfluenza virus and also by a bacteria—*Bordetella Bronchiseptica*, however, the exact cause may vary.
>
> This condition would rarely lead to complications or death only in animals with a weakened immune system. In summary, kennel cough is not much different than a cold that most of us catch from time to time and cure by rest and tea.

Many boarding facilities, doggy daycares, trainers, and groomers require a kennel cough or Bordetella vaccine be given to dogs before they visit. If the vaccine is given 7–10 days prior to the visit your Beagle may develop immunity, but it's also possible that he will get a case of kennel cough just from receiving the vaccine. Quite often the vaccine is given to dogs on the day they enter a facility; it is not possible for them to have immediate immunity due to the vaccine.

The majority of businesses that request the vaccine probably do so to avoid liability in case a client's dog develops kennel cough. If you offer to sign a waiver the business owner may not object to your dog skipping the Bordetella vaccine.

Because of the risk of your Beagle developing kennel cough symptoms from the vaccine alone, as well as the extremely low risk of his developing any severe symptoms from the disease, it should not be considered an essential vaccine.

Vaccinations

Beagles should be vaccinated as puppies for the three most common deadly dog diseases: Parvovirus, Distemper, and Adenovirus 2; these

Vaccination Schedule for Dogs*

Disease	Initial Vaccination	Boosters
Parvo, Distemper, and Adenovirus 2 are core vaccines which should be given to all puppies.		
Distemper	6 weeks	8 weeks; 16 weeks
Adenovirus 2**	6 weeks	8 weeks; 16 weeks
Parvovirus	6 weeks	8 weeks; 16 weeks
Rabies	12–16 weeks	Second vaccination at about one year of age, depending upon local and state ordinances, with annual to triennial shots for the rest of the dog's life.
The following vaccinations may only need to be given if local risk is high for the disease.		
*Bordetella***	6 weeks	8 weeks
Coronavirus	6 weeks	8 weeks
Hepatitis	6 weeks	8 weeks; 16 weeks
Leptospirosis	6 weeks	8 weeks; 16 weeks
Parainfluenza	6 weeks	8 weeks; 16 weeks

*The vaccination schedule will typically vary from one veterinarian to another, and within different locations of the country where risks may differ. Vaccinations are now available for Lyme disease, which may be recommended for the hunting/field trial Beagle. Please consult your veterinarian.
**In part responsible for the "kennel cough" syndrome (see page 62).

vaccines are known as core vaccines. Rabies vaccines are required by law to be given yearly or every three years. All other vaccines are less critical for your Beagle depending upon the area you live in and the severity of the disease. Vaccines do not need to be routinely given to dogs for diseases which are rarely contracted and can be easily treated by a veterinarian. Properly handled and administered high titer vaccines should confer lifetime immunity for the three core diseases. Titer blood tests will confirm if your dog has immunity to specific diseases and can be done before booster vaccines are given. Just as human adults do not need yearly boosters for childhood diseases that they have already been vaccinated against, dogs do not need to have a yearly booster once they have immunity to a disease.

Routine vaccination of sick or immune compromised individuals, as well as geriatric dogs is a highly questionable practice.

Adverse reactions to vaccines can include shock, depression/lethargy, itching, and even death in rare cases. If your Beagle has a severe reaction you should have him seen immediately by your veterinarian.

Canine Diseases

Distemper

Canine distemper is a viral disease that strikes mainly young dogs but also can infect other animals, including raccoons, coyotes, skunks, and wolves. It poses no danger to humans.

The first symptoms of distemper are visible about five to eight days after the virus invades the body. At first, only the mucous membranes are affected. Common symptoms are coughing, sneezing, nasal discharge, teary eyes, and sometimes diarrhea and vomiting.

The virus then proceeds to invade other tissues and do damage there. At that point, a secondary bacterial infection can significantly worsen the disease picture. The lungs are particularly susceptible. Bronchitis, pneumonia, and pleuritis are possible. These complications can be so serious as to be fatal.

The most serious form of the disease appears after three to five days. The dog's temperature runs as high as 103° to 105°F (39.5°–40.5°C); immediate medical attention is required. Without it, distemper enters the nervous system. This brings about a variety of symptoms, ranging from lameness to muscle spasms. In most cases, infections of the nervous system are fatal. Few dogs recover completely and most survivors are left with a disability.

No medicines are effective against distemper. Frequently, antibiotics are prescribed to fight the secondary bacterial infection, but these antibiotics have no effect whatever on the virus. The only medication for distemper is prevention, brought about by a well-planned vaccination schedule.

Authorities are virtually unanimous in advising that puppies be vaccinated against distemper by the time they are six weeks old, as well as a booster shot two to four weeks later.

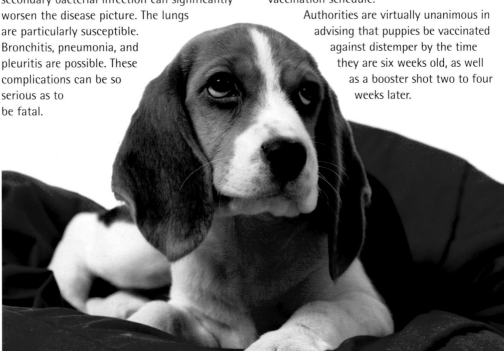

Hepatitis

Hepatitis is a virus disease that is sometimes fatal. The infected animal loses its appetite, runs a fever, emits a bloody diarrhea, or vomits. It is quite obvious that the dog has abdominal pains.

Sometimes the disease has a rapid course: One day the dog looks completely healthy and the next day it is dead. It is clear that a veterinarian needs to be consulted immediately. He or she will administer antibiotics, intravenous fluids, and vitamins and may provide a blood transfusion or infuse other fluids.

Hepatitis can be prevented with a modified live vaccine, which is commonly provided along with distemper vaccine. This is a remarkably effective vaccine. It is thought that a single injection provides lifelong immunity. After a booster shot, the dog may be generally sluggish, loses his appetite, and runs an elevated temperature. You may need to consult a veterinarian if after a few days his condition doesn't improve or worsens.

Dog Diseases and Humans?

Yes! Diseases transmissible to humans include leptospirosis and rabies (if a rabid dog inflicts a bite). Therefore, it is always advisable to consult a veterinarian whenever it is unclear from what illness a dog is suffering.

Leptospirosis

This kidney infection is caused by bacterial organisms (*Leptospira* species). It is infectious to humans and occurs in cattle and rats as well as dogs, raccoons, swine, and many other mammals.

The sick Beagle has an obvious temperature, completely loses its appetite, has abdominal pains, vomits, loses weight, frequently shows

Rabies Reminder

There is no treatment for rabies once symptoms have developed in man or dog! Vaccinations against rabies are mandatory for all dogs (see Vaccination Schedule, page 63). This will protect your beloved animal and thus you and your family from this potentially fatal disease.

a weakness of the hind legs, has diarrhea, and drinks a large volume of water.

The veterinarian administers antibiotics, the necessary fluids, and vitamins. To allow the kidneys the chance to heal properly, the veterinarian may perform peritoneal dialysis.

Vaccination may prevent this disease; however, there are several strains of Leptospirosis, not all are included in the vaccine. The disease spreads by contact with the urine of an infected animal or by drinking or swimming in contaminated water.

After a vaccination, dogs can often exhibit the same symptoms as after a hepatitis booster. Due to the high rate of adverse reactions and high rate of vaccine failure, you may want to consider skipping this vaccine.

Rabies

Rabies, or "hydrophobia," is caused by a fatal virus that is highly concentrated in the saliva of rabid animals, such as foxes, skunks, bats, raccoons, cats, and dogs. The virus was first identified by Louis Pasteur in 1881. Rabies is an acute infectious disease of the central nervous system. Many, if not all, warm-blooded animals can spread this disease, which is endemic in many countries. Rabies-free countries, such as Britain, Australia, and New Zealand, impose strict quarantine regulations to avoid its spread, and even a current vaccination certificate is required when shipping your Beagle across some state lines (ask your veterinarian).

No warm-blooded animal will get rabies until it is bitten by a rabid animal, or infected by a rabid animal's saliva through an open wound. In man, early symptoms include nausea, fever, malaise, and sore throat. Increased salivation and extreme sensitivity of the skin to temperature changes, of the eyes to light, and of the ears to sound are signs very important to early diagnosis.

The incubation period of the rabies virus is usually between 10 and 120 days, but sometimes up to six months, depending on the location of the bite and the time it takes the virus to reach the brain.

There are two types of rabies: *dumb rabies* (the dog is far from active, the mouth often hangs open, and there is apt to be a peculiar look in the eyes) and *furious rabies*. In the latter the dog is snappy and irritable, becomes restless, and wanders off to hide in dark places. It often howls and usually attacks and/or bites any human or animal that crosses his path. Seek veterinary attention immediately, and if anyone is bitten by a suspect dog (or other warm-blooded animal), clean the wound with soap or disinfectant at once and consult a physician without delay. Prompt action can save a life!

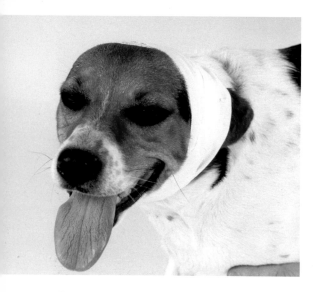

ment, you may be able to avoid putting your pet at risk for more serious medical problems.

First Aid

Bites

Beagles are not the biting type, but they do sometimes bite humans or another animal. Males or females that are kept together in a kennel have been known to inflict painful bites on each other, frequently involving a bitten foot or a torn ear. Bite wounds, including those on the ears, can bleed severely.

If your Beagle suffers a small wound, wash it with a mild antiseptic. If it needs stitches, or if a wound seems to heal slowly, consult your veterinarian.

Insect Stings

Beagles are extremely playful, and they love to chase bees and wasps. No wonder that Beagles are subject now and then to a painful sting! Wash the stung area with a strong solution of bicarbonate of soda. Be sure to consult a veterinarian for stings on or near the nose, mouth, tongue, or eyes.

Frostbite

Frostbite, which makes the animal shiver and look sleepy, is rare in dogs, even in hunting hounds like Beagles. If they have been outside in freezing weather for a long time, however, it is still quite possible that the margins of the ear, the tail, or the scrotum may be affected by frostbite. If you suspect this, put your Beagle in a warm room. Place a hot water bottle (in a cover) in her dog bed or use an electric pad or blanket if available. This helps raise the body

Parvovirus

The parvovirus primarily attacks the bone marrow, immune system, and gastrointestinal tract, but it can also damage the heart. It is a serious killer, especially of puppies, but it can bring death to an unvaccinated or untreated dog of any age. Puppies with this disease can suffer from severe dehydration because of profuse bloody, watery diarrhea and vomiting, and may die within 48 hours of onset.

While good veterinary care can save some parvovirus victims, immunization is a much better course of action.

Coronavirus

This contagious disease can cause severe diarrhea with watery, loose, foul-smelling, bloody stool. It may leave a dog in such a weakened condition that parvovirus or other infections may occur. Immunization by vaccine is the preferred course. By preventing this ail-

temperature. Warm the affected parts with your hands or use a moist, warm towel (note that I said *warm*, not *hot!*). Under no circumstances should you rub or squeeze! Give the Beagle warm liquids to drink, and check the rectal temperature every hour.

If the animal is unconscious, consult a veterinarian immediately.

Disorders of the Eyes

If your Beagle suddenly closes its eyelids, it may have sand or other foreign bodies in the eye. Rinse the eye or eyes carefully with eyewash. If none is available, use tap water that has been boiled, cooled, and, if possible, filtered. Apply with a plastic syringe, which is available in the drugstore. Be sure not to touch the eyeball in the process. When you rinse, be sure you use more than enough rinsing liquid.

If your Beagle continues to squeeze her eyelids (or there is no marked improvement), consult your veterinarian because you are probably dealing with an infection of the mucous tissue or a foreign body. Such an infection often

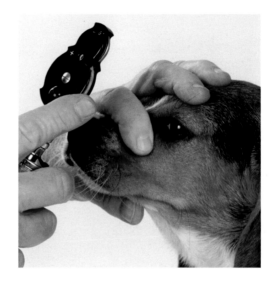

results from strong drafts—for example, if your Beagle was permitted to put her head out of the window of a moving vehicle.

Any eye irritation causes heavy tearing, but a heavy flow of tears can also be caused by a blockage in the tear ducts. A veterinarian can flush away the blockage. Stick to the following

rule: If excessive tearing persists longer than a day, consult your veterinarian. A number of eye infections and disorders, such as glaucoma, should be treated only by a veterinarian. The so-called "cherry eye" concerns the prolapsed gland of the third eyelid, and is a common problem in Beagles. Corrective surgery can tack the gland back into place.

Temperature and Heart Rate

As soon as the body temperature of a dog exceeds 103°F (39.5°C), it has a fever. This doesn't always mean that it is sick. The body temperature may rise somewhat because of excitement, or from riding in a hot car, among other reasons. You can take the temperature rectally.

To help establish whether your Beagle may require a veterinarian's attention, you can also check the pulse on the left front paw, or on the upper inside of the thigh. Place your finger lightly on one of these spots for one minute and count the number of beats.

A healthy, grown dog has a pulse rate or heart rate of about 100 beats a minute. Puppies will usually have a heart rate up to 180 beats per minute.

Euthanasia

If your Beagle remains healthy and avoids serious accidents, the end of his days will probably occur between his twelfth and fifteenth year.

An aged Beagle tends to rise with difficulty and walk slowly. When lying down, he may collapse and remain where he hits the floor. The lenses of his eyes become opaque with cataract development; that and bumping into recently moved furniture indicate a degree of blindness. He may exhibit deafness, urinary control may fail, and he may have fecal accidents. More serious problems may result such as arthritic joints, loss of appetite, kidney failure, and attitude changes. Some of these geriatric changes may be relieved by your veterinarian.

The aging process in Beagles tends to be gradual, in contrast to the situation with large dogs, which can go from exuberance to infirmity within months. If no serious illness or infirmities occur, you can continue to enjoy your last years with your pet.

There are cases, however, in which an animal develops so many ailments that he requires almost constant attention without any clear sign that he will soon die naturally. In such cases, you must seriously consider the possibility of euthanasia. Discuss the situation with your veterinarian. Let him or her give you a professional opinion about the quality of your Beagle's life. If your Beagle is obviously suffering, his quality of life needs to be considered and euthanasia may be the best remaining course of action. It is always better to end his suffering too soon, rather than too late.

At this point, your dog has been your loyal friend and companion for many years, so it is only fair that you stay with him to his last breath and heartbeat. Your dog has the right to spend his last moments in your company.

You need not be afraid of the leave-taking. Death in the office of your veterinarian is a far from scary event. The veterinarian will use personal skills and medications to calm your Beagle, so that he first falls into a deep sleep.

At that point, the breathing becomes shallower and the heart beats more slowly. The dog remains asleep until the end.

You will be left with an empty, sad feeling. After all, your faithful companion through the years has disappeared from your life forever. All you have are the memories.

It is natural to grieve the loss of your companion. Dwell on the pleasant memories you have of him and over time the hole he left behind will heal.

OBEDIENCE TRAINING USING MARKERS

Marker or clicker training (also known as operant conditioning) is a highly effective training method based on positive reinforcement to clearly communicate with animals. Marker training has been used for decades by animal trainers to achieve remarkable results with over 140 species including whales, bears, lions, chickens, dogs, cats, and humans.

Marker training gives you a positive method of telling your dog the instant that he does something you like, as well as providing a non-punishment method of telling your dog the instant he does something you don't like. It will also give you a method to tell him that you like what he is doing and you want him to continue doing that action. When you can communicate these things with your dog he will want to participate with you and he can be trained to do almost anything.

Marker training uses a verbal marker such as "YES" while clicker training uses a small mechanical clicker to communicate with your dog.

You can use marker or clicker training with 8-week-old puppies or with difficult older rescue dogs. This method of training is non-confrontational so it works very well with untrained dogs, dogs that need to be retrained or difficult dogs.

Marker training is operant conditioning, which forms an association between a behavior and a consequence. When a dog does an action that we like the consequence is a high value treat or toy that the dog really loves. If a dog does not perform a behavior the consequence is no reward, this is a negative reinforcer. If the dog wants the high value reward he must repeat the exercise with the correct response. In traditional compulsion training the consequence of a negative behavior is a correction, this results in dogs that are afraid to try to figure out what the handler wants or to think on their own because if they make a mistake they get a correction. Dogs will try hard to please and they enjoy working with their trainer if they are not corrected for mistakes during training. Corrections are never used until you get to the advanced stages of training when you are sure the dog knows your commands but is refusing to comply.

Rewards must be something that your dog really loves, and most Beagles love food. Some Beagles may prefer a special toy that is only brought out at training time. Treats such as bacon, cheese, steak, or freeze-dried liver would probably all be high value to your dog. You can offer two different treats at a time and see which one he eats first. When training use his favorite one, or mix several kinds together so that he randomly gets his favorite treat. Treats should be soft and about the size of a dried pea; if they are hard many dogs will cough

them up; if they are too big you will have to wait while the dog chews; if they are too small the dog may not stay focused on you.

You can carry your training treats in your hands, in your training vest pockets, or in a bait bag. If using a bait bag, ideally you should carry it behind your back and reach back with both hands at the same time to retrieve the treats. You should randomly change which hand offers the treats. If you always use the same front pocket, and the same hand to reach for and deliver the treats your dog will become fixated on your pocket and hand rather than the marker, which will make training more difficult.

If your Beagle has a low food drive (this would be unusual for a Beagle) you can wait to feed him his regular meal after training. If he still isn't motivated by food, fast him for a day before training. Fasting a healthy adult dog for a day won't hurt him and it will increase his food drive—making training easier.

To see if your dog prefers food treats or a toy hold one in each hand and see which one he wants the most (he will stare at it, jump, or bark toward that hand). In order to use a toy as a reward the dog must first be trained:

1. That the toy is only fun when the handler plays too.

2. That he must give up the toy with one command.

3. If the handler releases the toy the dog must bring it back.

Despite popular opinion, dogs don't do things just to make their owner feel good, they do things to make themselves feel good, comfortable, or to eliminate discomfort. The key to successful training is to make it easy for the dog to give us a behavior we want in order to receive a reward he enjoys. It is extremely rare for a dog to work his best for only handler praise. If you think your dog is the rare one who works best for pets and kisses you should make a comparison between his response to praise and his response to really high-value treats (grain-based dog biscuits don't count); the reward he really works for is the one you should use.

The most effective training involves keeping the consequence of a behavior within ½ second to 1½ seconds of a behavior, this is easiest to do with markers. The instant the dog performs the desired behavior it is marked with a YES, or a click, the reward can then follow a few seconds later; in this way the dog takes a snapshot of the moment in time when you marked his behavior and he knows which behavior you liked. The mark is a bridge that tells the dog "I like that behavior and a reward is on its way." It is very important to say YES only one time when your dog gives you the right behavior; to repeat it over and over again will only confuse him. You must also be sure to give him a reward every time you say yes, even if you marked the wrong behavior; he must know that the mark means he will get a reward.

Negative markers allow you to tell your dog that he just made a mistake, it is not a correction, it's communication. NO, NOPE, or OOPS can be used for a negative marker; be sure to say it in a neutral tone, not a harsh or grumpy tone. When your dog hears the negative marker he will learn that he must correctly repeat the exercise to get his high-value reward.

Dogs trained with markers learn to think and solve problems. When one behavior doesn't work they will try another behavior; if that one doesn't work they keep trying until they figure

Practice Before Training

You will have an easier time training your dog if you first practice marker training (using people treats like grapes, nuts, or chocolate) with a friend or family member who is cooperative and has a sense of humor. You will quickly learn how to improve your marker timing and training methods. Be sure to trade off where one of you is the "dog" and one of you is the trainer. The idea is to make it as easy as possible for the "dog" to figure out what you want without talking to them. You should only say YES, GOOD, NOPE and then praise at the end of the exercise. Two things that are very helpful for the "dog" is for the trainer to look at the target, and to deliver the reward close to the target. When you see how long it takes an intelligent human to figure out the training exercises you will have more patience to wait for your Beagle to think it through.

out what you want. Negative markers allow dogs to learn from their mistakes, without correcting them during the process.

To begin training your Beagle you will teach him 5 words; these words can be used with every exercise you want to train your dog.

1. READY? or **ARE YOU READY?** This tells your dog that you are about to start a training session; when the dog engages with you or starts to offer behaviors you should always reward him. If your dog doesn't feel like playing with you on some days you should put him in his kennel or take him for a walk. When dogs understand engagement they will view their human as their own treat dispenser, all they have to do is some silly exercises to get their high-value treat or toy. If your Beagle is very laid back you may need to teach him how to engage with you; you can use an excited happy voice, back away from him as you offer a treat, and have a little party when he responds to you.

2. YES is the positive marker used to bridge the time between the behavior we want and

the delivery of the reward. YES is also used as a release command and tells your dog he can get his treat or toy from you after he has done something right. It is important to say YES only once for each right behavior. If you get excited and say it several times you will only confuse your dog. Make a point to say YES once and then at the end of the exercise add GOOD BOY to praise him.

Before you start marking behaviors you must first CHARGE THE MARK so the dog understands that YES means a treat is on its way. To do this make sure you have your dog's attention, say YES, then hand a treat to your dog (be sure that you have a tiny pause between YES and when your hand moves to get the treat or to give it to your dog); repeat this 15 or more times until your dog understands that YES always means a reward is on its way.

NO MARK is important in that it communicates to your dog that he hasn't yet given you the behavior you want. It's a non-stressful way to tell him that he needs to keep trying.

If your Beagle doesn't seem to be understanding what you want him to do you need to be patient and give him a little while to figure it out.

3. GOOD is the word that tells your dog you like what he is doing and you want him to continue doing it; it adds duration to a command. If you are teaching SIT STAY you would not mark the dog when he sat because the mark is also the release. You can say GOOD as many times as you need to get the dog to continue what he is doing; your dog will learn that if he continues doing exactly what he is doing he will get the reward at some time in the future. You can help your dog learn the meaning of the word GOOD by saying good when you are praising him, petting him, or feeding him.

4. NO or **NOPE** is the negative marker word. It lets your dog know that he just made a mistake and he will have to do the exercise over again. NOPE should be said in a pleasant or neutral tone so the dog knows you are not mad, and that he is not going to get a correction, it only means that he needs to correctly repeat the exercise to get his high-value reward. If your dog really loves the reward he will figure out pretty quickly that NOPE means he gets to do it again.

5. DONE or **BREAK** is the word that tells your dog that the training session is over for now; it can be done for ten minutes or for the rest of the day. When you say DONE the food and toys are put away until the next training session; then show your empty hands to your dog. He will soon learn that DONE means the training session is over.

Body Language vs. Words

Dogs are very good at reading body language. Most people think that dogs know the words they are saying, but they are actually just reading the person's body language. By varying your training location (kitchen, living room, yard, etc.) and your body position (facing sideways or backwards, moving, sitting, etc.) you will help your dog learn the command words.

YES Marker or Clicker Mark

When marking a behavior it is very important to always say YES the same way every time. If you cannot keep the tone and inflection of your voice the same every time you mark, it may change what your dog thinks you are saying. Using a marker word has several advantages over a clicker: you almost never lose your voice, you don't need a free hand to operate it, your voice will carry farther during distance training than a click, and your voice is distinctive and easily identified by your dog in a crowd of other marker trainers. A clicker has the advantage of sounding the same every time you click. You should use a clicker if you have trouble keeping your voice consistent when you are stressed or excited during a training situation. You can teach your Beagle to respond equally well to YES and to a click, just charge the clicker as well as YES and then alternate the two at different training sessions.

upbeat verbal praise). If your dog knows that he will get extra treats and praise when he gets something right he will be more likely to keep trying to figure out the more difficult exercises, rather than giving up when he doesn't understand it right away. It's important to end your training on a good note by jackpotting the last MARK before the DONE or BREAK command.

If you are in the habit of being dull and boring with treat and praise delivery during training you will probably get dull and boring results from your Beagle. If you don't feel like getting excited about training, you can either fake it for your dog's sake or train another day when you're in better spirits.

Distractions

When your Beagle is distracted he won't learn as quickly as he does with no distractions, and he may not even try to work with you. Your dog may be very cooperative and obedient at home but as soon as he is in a different or more distracting environment he will seem to forget everything he knows. To overcome this you need to gradually increase the distractions your dog is working around. Start with small distractions and when your dog can ignore them move on to slightly more distracting situations. If you find yourself in a situation where your dog is not doing as well as you thought he should be doing you need to go back to a less challenging environment. It is important to only change one thing at a time when increasing distractions; you can change the distraction level, or you can ask for a new behavior—if you do both at the same time you are almost guaranteeing that your dog will fail.

Jackpotting Rewards

When your Beagle is working through, or has completed, a training exercise and you want him to know that you're very happy with his work, you still only MARK one time but you can jackpot the reward by giving him several high-value treats (you can also give him some

Targeting

A good place to start marker training is targeting (a target stick—a stick with a small ball on the end—is a popular targeting tool and is available at many pet stores). Hold the stick away from your side, when your Beagle looks at it mark and reward him. You can deliver the reward at the ball on the end of the stick to speed his learning. Repeat until your dog knows to look at the stick when you hold it out. When he takes one step toward the stick, mark and reward. Then mark two steps, and then sniffing the stick, and finally touching the stick with his nose.

When you look at the target it helps your Beagle figure out what you want him to touch, as does delivering the reward as close to the target as possible.

Targeting is a very useful exercise because it can be used as the foundation for many other behaviors—such as teaching your dog to go to his bed, into his crate, retrieving, and recall. You can use targeting to teach the hand touch command, which is useful for redirecting your dog away from any distractions during walks.

Luring During Marker Training

Luring is when you show your dog the treat before an exercise and then use it to lure or guide his movements through an exercise. Some people call this a bribe, but it should be looked at as a faster way of helping the dog learn what you want. After you have charged the mark you teach your Beagle to follow the lure by letting him smell the lure in your hand (but don't let him have it), then move your hand away from him. As he follows the food

hand, you mark the follow and open your hand to release the food. He will get the idea pretty quickly. It is always easier to lure a dog toward you, so you should start with getting him used to luring away from your body.

Dogs will always follow a physical lure/cue over a verbal command, so you must have a plan to phase out the lure as soon as possible.

Lures are faded by adding a verbal command for the behavior. You start this process when the dog is responding well to the gesture for the lure; at this point you give the command and immediately offer the lure gesture, then mark and reward the behavior. Repeat this 10, 20, 50 times, or as many times as you think your dog needs. You can test him by giving the command without the lure, if he performs the behavior he has learned the command. If your dog hesitates and doesn't offer the behavior just say NOPE, reposition him to where he

was before the command was given and then repeat the command and gesture another 10–20 times until you think he is ready for another test.

If your Beagle hesitates and doesn't correctly respond to the command DO NOT add the gesture; this will teach him to wait for the gesture.

Some of the first exercises you can use luring for is when you teach your Beagle to sit, lay down, and come.

Baby Steps

By breaking a complicated training exercise into small parts (baby steps) that your Beagle can easily understand, you will make it very easy for her to learn complicated exercises. As an example, if you wanted to train her to go across the yard and put her front feet in a bowl, you would break it down into several steps: start with the bowl and dog close to you and then teach your dog to look at the bowl, step to the bowl, touch the bowl with her foot, put one foot in the bowl, put two feet into the bowl, then do the exercise farther and farther away from you until she can go across the yard and put both front feet into the bowl.

Any time you find that your dog is having trouble with a training exercise see if it's possible to break it down into even smaller parts to make it easier to understand.

When to End a Training Session

Always end your training sessions on a good note when your dog still has energy and she is concentrating on what you're asking her to do—ideally she has just successfully completed a training exercise. If the exercise you're working on is a difficult one and your dog is having trouble or stops trying and you feel it's time to end the session, just ask your dog to do something simple that you are 100% certain

she knows and enjoys doing, such as the hand touch. Some dogs will only be able to train for a short session of a few minutes; others will be able to train for 15–20 minutes at a time. When you are just learning how to marker train it's a good idea to put only about 20 treats in your bait bag; when they are gone it's time to end the session.

Teaching Sit

After you have practiced marker training with a human (this is an important step, do not skip it) you are ready to start training your Beagle. Get your Beagle's attention (say her name if it helps) then CHARGE THE MARK; when she understands that YES means a treat is on its way it's time to move on to the next step. Hold the treat in your closed hand so your Beagle can smell it (do not give her the treat) then slowly move your hand just over her head so that she has to look up at it. Pretty soon she will decide to sit. The second she sits MARK and reward. Repeat the exercise several times (gradually phasing out the treat in your hand) until she knows that your hand over her head means that she should sit. This is when you are ready to link the command with the gesture. Say SIT just before you move your hand over her head; repeat this 10–50 times. When you think she is ready test her with just the SIT command, if she hesitates say NOPE, start over and go back to saying SIT and then the gesture; repeat 10–20 times and test her again with just SIT.

You can help your dog learn the SIT command outside of training sessions when you see her sit on her own; as soon as her rear end touches the ground say SIT.

Look

Look At Me or **Look** is an important command for your dog to know as it can help you keep or regain your Beagle's attention in distracting environments. Use luring to get your dog to look into your eyes, then you MARK and reward. Continue with the training progression that I have outlined for SIT until you can get your dog to reliably respond every time you say LOOK.

Teaching Down

If you have already taught your Beagle to SIT and LOOK you should have no trouble with DOWN. Luring is very helpful to get your dog to lay down. Start by bringing the treat close to her nose; then bring it down low and away so she follows it down. If she always wants to walk forward instead of laying down you can sit on the floor and lure her under your bent legs. The second her belly is on the floor you MARK and reward. Continue with the same steps you used to teach sit.

To learn more about marker training visit *www.leerburg.com* for training articles, books and videos. I would recommend two DVDs: *The Power of Training Dogs with Markers* and *The Power of Training Dogs with Food—with Michael Ellis.*

UNDERSTANDING BEAGLES

The Beagle belongs to the hound breeds, which can be split into two groups: (1) The scent hounds or scent followers and (2) the sight hounds or sight hunters.

The Beagle is by far the best known representative of the scent followers and one of the oldest representatives of the scent-following tracking dogs. The breed probably dates back to pre-Roman times.

In the United States, we recognize two sizes of Beagles: 13 inches or under, and over 13 but under 15 inches. The typical weight for a Beagle is between 20–25 pounds.

Dog experts often say, correctly, that the Beagle is a carbon copy of the Harrier and the English Foxhound. Both these breeds are considerably larger than the Beagle, especially the English Foxhound.

Although a Beagle may have any hound color, most members of the breed are black, white, or tan, with different combinations and markings. The coat is close and of medium length and will remain glossy with good daily care. The tail of a healthy Beagle is carried gaily, but not curled squirrel style; the ears are set at eye level, drop beside the cheeks, and have "fine leather." The skull is domed and moderately wide, with an indication of peak. The medium-length muzzle should not be snippy.

If you want to acquire a Beagle and know a dependable pet store or breeder, fine. If not, start by contacting your veterinarian and registries such as the AKC for assistance (see address on page 92). The AKC will give you the address of the headquarters of the local Beagle club and names of breeders in your area.

Remember that the Beagle has remained popular through the years, despite the competition, because of its many excellent qualities and valued traits. Two of its very outstanding qualities are certainly endurance and courage. It is difficult, perhaps impossible, to find a breed that surpasses the Beagle on these points. The Beagle in the field is almost as well known in America as in Europe, although we know the breed somewhat better as a house pet.

As a house pet, the Beagle still distinguishes itself by several excellent qualities. As I said earlier, Beagles and children are almost inseparable, and the charming and intelligent Beagles are also generally affectionate toward other pets. They are always ready to be on the go, and from excitement and pure joy they often sound their lovely hound voice.

You will have to set limits on this enthusiastic vocalization if you keep a Beagle in the city, as you don't want trouble with the neighbors. If you acquire the dog when it is young, you can train it fairly easily even though a Beagle, as a natural hunter, derives an unimaginable deal of pleasure from a loud howling session now and then. This is particularly true if it is left alone, but if you start when the dog is young, you shouldn't run into any serious problems.

The Beagle is definitely a suitable city hound. It certainly loves to be outside often and will thankfully accept any opportunity to be taken for a walk or to romp out-of-doors. As you walk through the streets, you can depend on the Beagle's natural calm as well as its proverbial loyalty. Believe me, the Beagle doesn't care at all about bad weather or rough terrain; you can take your dog wherever you want, secure in the knowledge that nothing will wear it down.

If you are a hunter, the Beagle is hard to beat. Almost any type of upland game arouses its interest, including cottontail rabbit, squirrel, and pheasant, which are its favorites. If you train the Beagle properly, you can derive an enormous amount of pleasure from your helper. Professional trainers often can be of indispensable assistance in developing your Beagle as a hunter.

History

Legend has it that Beagles, those "merry little hounds with big hearts," descended from hounds used by King Arthur and his knights. Some say their ancestors came to England with William the Conqueror. It isn't easy, however, to establish exactly when the breed first made its appearance. It is known that the ancient Greeks used so-called scenting hounds for the hunt 400 years or so before Christ. The dogs, which were of several different breeds, hunted in packs with their keepers. In England and Wales this type of hunt was also known about 1400 A.D. The pack consisted not only of scent followers but also included sight hounds, such as greyhounds. In fact, it wasn't until 1550 that people started differentiating among the various types of scent hounds. For example, people trained the large hounds, the so-called buck hounds, to hunt deer

and other large game. The small hounds were used to hunt hares, rabbits, and pheasants; and these small dogs were called beighs or Beagles, from the French beigle, meaning *small*.

This doesn't mean, however, that the dogs that were called Beagles 400 years ago were the same dogs we call Beagles today. Representations of Beagles from the sixteenth, seventeenth, and eighteenth centuries show that clearly. The dogs varied in height between 5 and 25 inches (13–63.5 cm).

In this connection, it's interesting to note that in the days of King Henry VIII (1491–1547) and even more so during the reign of his daughter, Elizabeth I (1558–1603), the then miniature Beagles were transported to the hunting fields in the panniers of saddles or in the pockets of hunting coats.

One supposes that the Beagle resulted from experiments in crossing the Harrier with the Southern hound. It is no surprise that in the "early days" Beagles were often called "little harriers." Over time, breeders selected the larger individuals from among these dogs, creating a breed that was 19 to 21 inches (48–53.5 cm) in height. Continuous selection, using, in turn, only the smallest individuals for breeding, gradually resulted in a dog of reduced size, a miniature breed called Queen Bess. These dogs proved to be too small for hunting, and they rapidly lost popularity. Breeders continued their experiments, and gradually the first "true" Beagle developed in two types: the shallow-flewed and the deep-flewed, depending on the depth of the upper lip. The first type is supposed to have

been the faster, and the second, the one with the more musical voice and the more assured manner.

The present-day Beagle received a number of characteristics from several other breeds. Its keen nose is supposedly derived from the Kerry Beagle, a miniature bloodhound, and all its other traits were acquired by crossing various foxhounds (harriers).

It wasn't until about 1860 that the first well-proportioned Beagles were introduced to the United States. One of the known participants was General Richard Rowett of Carlinville, Illinois, who brought several good representatives of the breed from England, including the now famous Rosey and Dolly.

Beagles were known in North America before then, but they were far from ideal individuals, especially in size. The dogs brought over by Rowett and others were used in a professional selective breeding program that resulted in superior Beagles within several years. They were able to meet all competitors, including those from England.

It wasn't until 1887, however, that the American/English Beagle Club was formed. The standard of the breed was drafted by General Rowett, Norman Elmore of Granby, Connecticut—famous for his marvelous Beagle Ringwood, which also came from England—and Dr. L. H. Twadell of Philadelphia, Pennsylvania. These gentlemen acquitted themselves so well of their task that their standard, with several minor changes, continues to be used today by the National Beagle Club of America. Even the standard used in England differs only slightly from the one devised by the three U.S. pioneers.

Shortly after the turn of the century, the interest in Beagles increased to an amazing extent, and many enthusiastic Beagle lovers had privately owned packs. Well-known are the Hempstead, Round Hill, Thurnfield, Rockridge, Dungannon, Somerset, Wolver, Piedmont, Old Westbury, and Windholme Beagles.

The first Beagle field trials were held November 4, 1890, at Hyannis, Massachusetts, and November 7, 1890, at Salem, New Hampshire. Mr. Frank Forest was the winner of the all-age stake for dogs 15 inches and under, and a dog called Tone, owned by the Glenrose Kennels, won the stake for bitches 15 inches and under. Belle Rose, owned by B. S. Turpin, was the winner of the stake for bitches 13 inches and under.

The next year, the number of entries was considerably larger, and from then on one can say that nothing could stop the popularity of the Beagle.

Beagles for Work in the Field

Several Beagle lovers have made a profession of training Beagles for work in the field. Many of these trainers now take their charges over a regular circuit of field trials. They are held almost every weekend throughout the country. Most successful field trial Beagles are taken hunting three to five days each week, to remain in top condition for competition.

Your Beagle club can tell you where you can find professional trainers. Remember that

generally they have more than enough business, so that you will need several names.

At bench shows and field trials, Beagles are divided into varieties by size: those not exceeding 13 inches in height at the withers, and those over 13 inches but not exceeding 15 inches.

The size varieties are then further subdivided into specific classes during competition: for field trials these would be 13-inch dogs, 13-inch bitches, 15-inch dogs, and 15-inch bitches. After reading our standards discussion (see pages 90–91), it will be clear that Beagles over 15 inches are automatically disqualified from competition.

It certainly would be well worth your time to visit a Beagle trial sometime, even if you don't like to hunt. During field trials, Beagles are run in braces (meaning pairs). The names of individual hounds are placed on single slips of paper and drawn from a receptacle, the first Beagle drawn running with the second hound drawn, and so on. After all braces have been run, the judges may call back any competing Beagle that they wish to see again and brace them in any manner they desire; often they make an animal run a second, third, or even fourth time. I have been at competitions where they made certain dogs run eight times. In the

end, all judges will have determined the best performers on that particular occasion.

Most generally, the cottontail rabbit is used as game, although it can happen that hares are used.

You can easily imagine that not all Beagles are equally adept at hunting; some may be easily distracted for one reason or another, or become nervous and perform poorly.

A young Beagle with true determination is just about the ideal hound. Its natural desire to hunt constitutes the germ for success, with the proper training. The trainer tries to get the Beagle to follow a comparatively cold trail until the quarry has gone to earth or has been caught. The young Beagle must be the type to enjoy working in rough, unknown territory, regardless of the weather.

It is safe to say that a good Beagle thrives on work, and the more it goes hunting with its master and its pack, the more it enjoys the chase. Even if you don't hunt, I think it will still be an unforgettable experience to see a pack of Beagles hunt. They truly deserve the name I heard somewhere: music makers of the meadows.

Beagle Shows

Every year there are local and regional shows for Beagle hounds. Using the breed standard as a basis, the judges evaluate and grade Beagles on their general appearance, physique, bearing, and behavior. Beagles are shown in two separate varieties. At the AKC point show, they are divided by sex into classes, from which the first-place winners advance to the Winners class. It is from the Winners class that the judge selects his one best class dog (and later

his one best class bitch) of each breed or variety to receive the point awards championship for the day.

The AKC judges place the hounds first through fourth in the classes, then select their Winners, Best of Breed, Best of Winners, and BOS (Best of Opposite Sex). Beagle shows (or dog shows, in general) offer a wealth of information. Manufacturers of dog foods offer samples of the latest brands, usually at no or little cost. Useful accessories for Beagle owners are also on display. Contacts with other Beagle owners are quickly formed, and a lively exchange of experience and information is

soon underway. The judges give tips and suggestions for the care and management of your Beagle.

If you would like to enter your Beagle in an AKC show, check the AKC events calendar for information, and then contact the show superintendent for a copy of the premium list which includes the appropriate entry forms. Blank official AKC entry forms can also be obtained from the AKC and kept on file for use in a pinch. But to enter any show you must mail the complete filled out and signed forms, with the appropriate fees, to the show superintendent for that specific show.

Description and Standard (AKC)

Head: The skull should be fairly long, slightly domed at occiput, with cranium broad and full.

Ears: Ears set on moderately low, long, reaching when drawn out nearly, if not quite, to the end of the nose; fine in texture, fairly broad—with almost complete absence of erectile power—setting close to the head, with the forward edge slightly inturning to the cheek—rounded at tip.

Eyes: Eyes large, set well apart; soft and houndlike; expression gentle and pleading; of a brown or hazel color.

Muzzle: Muzzle of medium length, straight and square-cut; the stop moderately defined.

Jaws: Level. Lips free from flews; nostrils large and open.

Defects: A very flat skull, narrow across the top; excess of dome; eyes small, sharp, and terrier-like or prominent and protruding; muzzle long, snippy or cut away decidedly below the eyes, or very short. Roman-nosed, or upturned, giving a dish-faced expression. Ears short, set on high or with a tendency to rise above the point of origin.

Body, neck, and throat: Neck rising free and light from the shoulders, strong in substance yet not loaded, of medium length. The throat clean and free from folds of skin; a slight wrinkle below the angle of the jaw, however, may be allowable.

Defects: A thick, short neck carried on a line with the top of the shoulders. Throat showing dewlap and folds of skin to a degree termed "throatiness."

Shoulders and chest: Shoulders sloping, clean, muscular, not heavy or loaded—conveying the idea of freedom of action with activity and strength. Chest deep and broad, but not broad enough to interfere with the free play of the shoulders.

Defects: Straight, upright shoulders. Chest disproportionately wide or with lack of depth.

Back, loin, and ribs: Back short, muscular, and strong. Loin broad and slightly arched, and the ribs well sprung, giving abundance of lung room.

Scale of Points

	Points	Total
Head		
Skull	5	
Ears	10	
Eyes	5	
Muzzle	5	25
Body		
Neck	5	
Chest and shoulders	15	
Back, loin, and ribs	15	35
Running Gear		
Forelegs	10	
Hips, thighs, and hind legs	10	
Feet	10	30
Coat	5	
Stern	5	10
		100

Varieties

There shall be two varieties: the 13 inch, which shall be for hounds not exceeding 13 inches in height, and the 15 inch, which shall be for hounds over 13 but not exceeding 15 inches in height.

Disqualification

Any hound measuring more than 15 inches shall be disqualified.

Defects: Very long, swayed, or roached back. Flat, narrow loin. Flat ribs.

Forelegs: Straight, with plenty of bone in proportion to size of the hound. Pasterns short and straight.

Feet: Close, round, and firm. Pad full and hard.

Defects: Out at elbows. Knees knuckled over forward or bent backward. Forelegs crooked or dachshund-like. Feet long, open, or spreading.

Hips, thighs, hind legs, and feet: Hips and thighs strong and well muscled, giving abundance of propelling power. Stifles strong and well let down. Hocks firm, symmetrical, and moderately bent. Feet close and firm.

Defects: Cowhocks or straight hocks. Lack of muscle and propelling power. Open feet.

Tail: Set moderately high; carried gaily, but not turned forward over the back; with slight curve; short compared with size of the hound; with brush.

Defects: A long tail. Teapot curve or inclined forward from the root. Rat tail with absence of brush.

Coat: A close, hard, hound coat of medium length.

Defects: A short, thin coat, or of a soft quality.

Color: Any true hound color.

General appearance: A miniature foxhound, solid and big for its inches, with the wear-and-tear look of the hound that can last in the chase and follow its quarry to the death.

INFORMATION

Organizations and Clubs

American Humane Association
1400 16th Street NW, Suite 360
Washington, DC 20036
(818) 501-0123
www.americanhumane.org

American Kennel Club
8051 Arco Corporate Drive, Suite 100
Raleigh, NC 27617-3390
(919) 233-9767
www.AKC.org

American Veterinary Medical Association
www.avma.org

Canadian Kennel Club
200 Ronson Drive, Suite 400
Etobicoke, Ontario M9W 5Z9
416-675-5511
www.ckc.ca

Canine Eye Registry Foundation (CERF)
1717 S. Philo Road, Suite 15
Urbana, IL 61802
(217) 693-4800
http://web.vmdb.org/home/CERF.aspx

Institute for Genetic Disease Control (GDC)
P.O. Box 177,
Warner, NH 03278
(603) 456-2350
http://gdcinstitute.org

International Boarding and Pet Services Association
3355 N. Academy Boulevard, #115
Colorado Springs, CO 80915
(877) 318-8172
www.ibpsa.com

National Beagle Club
http://clubs.akc.org/NBC/

National Dog Registry (tattoo, microchip)
9018 E. Wilson Road
Independence, MO 64053
1-800-NDR-DOGS (800-637-3647)
www.nationaldogregistry.com

Orthopedic Foundation for Animals (OFA)
2300 E. Nifong Boulevard
Columbia, MO 65201
573-442-0418
www.offa.org

Owner–Handler Association of America
Vickie Glickstein, membership chairperson
1901 Edge Hill Road
Abington, PA 19001
215-830-5068

Periodicals

AKC Gazette
www.akc.org/pubs/gazette/digital_edition.cfm

Dog Fancy Magazine
www.dogchannel.com/dog-magazines/dogfancy

Dog World
http://magazine-directory.com/Dog-World.htm

Books

In addition to the most recent edition of the official publication of the AKC, *The Complete Dog Book,* published by Howell Book House, Inc., in New York, the following publications contain useful information.

American Animal Hospital Association. *Encyclopedia of Dog Health and Care.* New York: The Philip Lief Group, Inc., 1994.

Baer, Ted. *Communicating with Your Dog.* Hauppauge, New York: Barron's Educational Series, Inc., 1994.

Billinghurst, Ian. *Give Your Dog a Bone.* Bathurst, NSW, Australia: Warrigal Publishing, 1993.

Clark, Ross D., and Joan R. Strainer. *Medical and Genetic Aspects of Purebred Dogs.* Fairway, Kansas, and St. Simons Island, Georgia: Forum Publications, Inc., 1994.

Coile, Caroline D. *Encyclopedia of Dog Breeds.* Hauppauge, New York: Barron's Educational Series, Inc., 1998.

Eldredge, Debra M., Liisa D. Carlson, Delbert G. Carlson, James M. Giffin. *Dog Owners Veterinary Handbook.* Hoboken, New Jersey. Wiley Publishing, Inc.: 2007

Fisher, Gail Tamases. *The Thinking Dog.* Wenatchee, Washington. Dogwise Publishing, 2009.

leerburg.com/dvdbooks.htm
Free dog training ebooks and videos

Lorenz, Konrad. *Man Meets Dog.* London and New York: Penguin Books, 1967.

O'Driscoll, Catherine. *Shock to the System.* Wenatchee, Washington. Dogwise Publishing, 2006.

Olsen, Lew. *Raw and Natural Nutrition for Dogs: The Definitive Guide to Homemade Meals.* Berkely, California: North Atlantic Books, 2010.

Pinney, Cristopher. *Guide to Home Pet Grooming.* Hauppauge, New York: Barron's Educational Series, Inc., 1990.

Pryor, Karen. *Getting Started: Clicker Training for Dogs.* Lydney, Gloucestersjore, U.K.: Ringpress Books , 2002.

Schultze, Kymythy, R. C.C.N., A.H.I. *Natural Nutrition for Dogs and Cats.* Carlsbad, California: Hay House, 1998.

Wrede, Barbara. *Civilizing Your Puppy.* Hauppauge, New York: Barron's Educational Series, Inc., 1992.

Important Note

This pet owner's guide tells the reader how to buy and care for Beagles. The author and the publisher consider it important to point out that the advice given in the book is meant primarily for normally developed puppies from a good breeder—that is, dogs of excellent physical health and good character.

Anyone who adopts a fully grown dog should be aware that the animal has already formed its basic impressions of human beings. The new owner should watch the animal carefully, including its behavior toward humans, and should meet the previous owner. If the dog comes from a shelter, it may be possible to get some information on the dog's background and peculiarities there. There are dogs that as a result of bad experiences with humans behave in an unnatural manner or may even bite. Only people who have experience with dogs should take in such an animal. Even well-behaved and carefully supervised dogs sometimes do damage to someone else's property or cause accidents. It is therefore in the owner's interest to be adequately insured against such eventualities, and we strongly urge all dog owners to purchase a liability policy that covers their dog.

Caution is further advised in the association of children with dogs, in meetings with other dogs, and in exercising the dog without a leash.

American Kennel Club, 8, 9, 92
  standard, 90–91
Anal sacs, 58–59

Baby, new, 35
Barking, 15, 24, 84
Beagle shows, 88–89
Bedding, 6, 29, 44
Biospot, 37
Bites, treating, 68
Boarding kennels, 31–32
Body language, 22, 77
Breeder, 7–11, 18, 21, 27, 54, 83
Brushing, 47
Buying considerations
  male vs. female, 5–7
  one or two dogs, 5

Canine distemper, 63, 64
Car, 21
Carbohydrates and fiber, 52
Chewing, 23, 28, 34
Children, 34–35, 84
Chlorophyll tablets, 9
Coat, 11, 29, 61, 83, 91
  care, 46–47
Coat or skin disorders, 57–58
Collar, 18, 19, 33, 36, 37
Commands, 81
Constipation, 58
Coronavirus, 68
Crate, 21, 23–24, 27–28, 33, 79

Diarrhea, 11, 27, 58, 60, 61, 64–66,
  68
Dog food, 49–51
  commercial, 52–53
  dry, semi-moist, canned, 54
  food variety, 53
  meals per day, 54
  raw meat and bone diet, 54
  senior or overweight dog, 54–55
  study, 50
Dog house, 29–30

Ear mites, 43
Ear tattoo, 18
Ears, 11, 42–43, 46–47, 58, 66, 90
Euthanasia, 71

Eye disorders, 69–70
Eyes, 11, 27, 47, 64, 66, 90

Fats and oils, 51–52
Female, 5–6, 9, 10, 11, 37
Fence, 7, 31
First Aid, 68–70
Fleas, 43
Food bowl, 24, 36
Foot care, 40
Frostbite, 68

Grooming, 36–37, 39–47

Heart rate, 70
Heartworms, 61–62
Hepatitis, 63, 65, 66
History of Beagles, 84–87
Hookworms and whipworms, 61
Housetraining, 22–24
Howling, 84
Hunting field trials, 45, 63, 68, 85,
  87–88
Hunting hound, 27, 42, 84

Identification tag, 37
Independent spirit, 5
Information, 92–93
Insect stings, 68

Kennel, 6, 10, 11
  boarding, 31–32
Kennel cough, 62

Leash, 6, 22, 23, 33, 36
Leptospirosis, 63, 65–66
Lice, 43–44
Life span, 5
Lyme disease, 45, 63

Males, 5–6, 9
Marker vs. clicker mark, 77
Microchips, 18–19

Nails, 40–42

Paper training, 23
Parasites, external, 43–45
Parvovirus, 63, 68

Pedigree, 7, 9
Private spot, 27–29
Protein, 51
Puppy
  five to six weeks old, 10
  getting settled, 27
  selecting a, 6, 7, 11–18
  seven to eight weeks old, 9, 11
  taking home, 21
Puppy Aptitude Test, 12–13

Rabies, 63, 66–67
Registration certificate, 9
Rescue dog, 7
Rocky Mountain spotted fever, 45
Roundworms, 60–61
The run, 31

Sanitary napkins, 6
Security room, 33
Shampoo, 36
Size, 83, 85–87, 91
Space considerations, 7
Spray for paws, 37
Sun vs. shade, 30

Tapeworms, 59–60
Targeting, 79
Teeth, 39–40
Temperature, 70
Tethering, 23
Ticks, 44–45
Toys, 33–34
Training session end, 80–81
Training using markers, obedience,
  73–81
Traveling with Beagle, 32–33
Treat, luring with, 79–80
Treats, 22, 24, 33, 34, 35, 55, 73–81

Vaccinations, 7, 9, 31–32, 45, 62–63,
  66
Volhard Obedience Aptitude Test,
  14–16

Walking, 22, 24, 36, 37, 40, 55, 84
Washing, 46–47
Water, 11, 21, 30, 36, 55
Water bowl, 24, 36
Worms, 59–61